D1369503

Quiltmakers of Australia

CELEBRATING THE TRADITIONS

THE QUILT DIGEST PRESS

Simply the Best from NTC Publishing Group

Lincolnwood, Illinois U.S.A.

Managing Editor: Judy Poulos.
Photography: Andrew Payne, Andrew Elton, Jonathon Chester,
K. Schwerdtfeger, Roger Deckker, David Patterson, Neil Lorimer,
Stuart Hay, Michael Pugh, Image Makers ACT, Terrence Darcy.
Production Manager: Anna Maguire.
Design: Michele Withers.
Additional Layout: Lulu Dougherty, Sheridan Packer.
Picture Editor: Kirsten Holmes.
Manufactured in Singapore.

Library of Congress Cataloging-in-Publication Data

Fail, Karen.
    Quiltmakers of Australia : celebrating the traditions / Karen Fail.
        p. cm.
    1. Quilting--/Australia. 2. Quiltmakers--Australia. I. Title.
TT835.F32 1996
746.46'092'294--dc20   96-1382
                                                              CIP

First published in the United States in 1996 by The Quilt Digest Press,
a division of NTC Publishing Group, 4255 West Touhy Avenue,
Lincolnwood (Chicago), Illinois 60646-1975, U.S.A.
© J.B. Fairfax Press Pty Limited 1995, 1996

First Published in Australia by J.B. Fairfax Press Pty Limited,
80-82 McLachlan Avenue, Rushcutters Bay, NSW 2011.

ISBN 0-8442-2607-6

Acknowledgments

My thanks to the wonderful quiltmakers who allowed me to invade
their homes, with lots of photographic equipment and many questions,
and still allowed me to call them my friends.
And to Andrew Payne, my photographer, whose enthusiasm
was so encouraging.
J.B. Fairfax Press and my editor Judy Poulos were so enthusiastic
about this project, and I thank them for their commitment.
My family have been, as usual, long-suffering and I cannot
thank them enough.
Thank you Paul, Rachel and Tim, Emma and Abby.

Contents

1850s remembered

JUDY DAY

10

Awash with colour

JUDY TURNER

16

Crazy about quilts

WENDY SACLIER

22

28

Chintz cutouts

MARJORIE PATTERSON

Gridded to perfection

KERRILYN GAVIN

34

40

Handmade by machine

LEE CLELAND

Contents

46

Magic masterpieces

KIM MCLEAN

54

Rags to riches

LYN INALL

60

Old quilts from new

BRIGITTE GIBLIN

68

Scrap happy

JAN URQUHART

74

Tiny treasures

VIRGINIA ENRIGHT

82

White on white

NARELLE GRIEVE

88

Picture perfect

ROBYN GINN

Introduction

I find what is happening in quiltmaking in Australia very exciting. With only a bare twenty years involvement in the worldwide revival of this craft, Australian quiltmakers have embraced every aspect of what has become one of the most popular forms of textile art in the world. While some have maintained the traditions passed down from previous generations, others have forged their own path, creating new directions beyond the traditions. What has happened as a result is a wonderful mix in Australian quilts of the traditional and innovative, the subdued and the outrageous, the ordered and the chaotic — all providing a visual feast for textile art lovers. Exhibitions abound and the excitement is contagious.

Margaret Rolfe, internationally known author of patchwork books, and Trudy Billingsley, famous worldwide for her wearable art, must take a large chunk of the credit for all this excitement. In the true tradition of patchworkers everywhere, they shared their enthusiasm for the quilts they had seen when visiting America in the 1970s and early 1980s, and they began teaching the basic skills of patchwork and quilting to aspiring quiltmakers who flocked to their classes. Little groups of quiltmakers began to get together to show their latest project and share ideas, and the rudimentary beginnings of the state guilds were born.

Not everyone attended classes. McCall's Needlework and Crafts *magazine, published in America, began to appear on the newsagents' shelves, and always featured a quilt. Many people were inspired to begin quiltmaking because of these early magazines. I had always admired the quilts, but never believed that I could make one, although I must admit it didn't occur to me to read the instructions. Now, when I look at my old copies of* McCall's Needlework and Crafts *that I can't bear to part with, I can't believe the simplicity of the quilts featured, and wonder what stopped me from beginning immediately. But, like many others, I eventually did begin, drawn by the possibility of creating something new and different.*

Perhaps this is the secret of the captivating quality of quiltmaking — the desire to be creative; to make something by which we can be remembered. So many of us, including many of the quilters in this book, made

decisions about our creativity when we were quite small. With creativity inexplicably linked to the ability to draw in our early years, many of us closed the door on the opportunity for self-expression long ago, simply because we couldn't draw a horse as well as the boy sitting next to us in year four.

Quiltmaking opens that door again, providing a wonderful avenue for self-expression. It doesn't seem to matter whether the quilts being made follow the traditions or are the most avant-garde pieces of textile art, the process of creating captures the quiltmaker, who becomes enthralled by the fabric, the colour, the processes and the textures. In the creative process, the quiltmakers reveal something of themselves, their quilts reflecting their character, their likes and dislikes, their passions and idiosyncrasies, their hopes and fears.

The quiltmakers featured in this book express their creativity by celebrating the traditions of quiltmaking. Often using techniques that have been practised by quiltmakers for centuries, they continue to refine and develop their work, creating wonderful quilts that truly reflect these traditions.

Very early in our history, the indigenous Australians had established a tradition of patchwork by crudely sewing skins together to form coverings for warmth. With colonisation, the traditions of British patchwork were brought to this country by Elizabeth Fry who provided the convict women with supplies to make quilts, thus giving them a way of earning a living in their new hostile environment. Many, however, failed to appreciate the treasures they were creating and, like much of the work done by women, quiltmaking was classified as domestic sewing and therefore of little importance, except for its utilitarian value. With so much domestic sewing a necessity, it is understandable that the women themselves undervalued their work and their own creativity. At the turn of the century, those women with more time on their hands were able to pursue the growing craze for fancywork. Crazy patchwork, introduced from England, became a popular way of displaying ornate and intricate stitches, a way of demonstrating a woman's prowess with the needle. Somehow this form of patchwork had more credibility because it was decorative rather than useful.

The English tradition of piecing over papers persisted during the twentieth century in Australia, and many people I meet tell stories of someone in their family who made hexagon quilts from scraps. Often, their first experience with patchwork was covering paper hexagons with fabric. This is also true for many of the quiltmakers featured in Celebrating the Traditions. Until very recently, this was the only method of patchwork taught in Australian schools and, in fact, when I first started quiltmaking in Singleton, New South Wales, in 1982, Joan Bowden from The Embroiderers' Guild came and taught a group of friends (including me) to patchwork. She taught piecing over papers, the only traditional patchwork with which she was familiar.

The influence of American traditions was not fully felt in Australia until the revival of interest in quiltmaking during America's Bicentenary celebrations in the 1970s. With renewed interest in their own heritage, Americans again embraced the craft that was born out of necessity when textiles were so scarce and bedcovers were essential. Women again began to enjoy the quiltmaking process, enticed by the interplay of design and colour, and inspired by the interaction with other quiltmakers. The excitement spread.

My interaction with the quiltmakers featured in Celebrating the Traditions has been extremely exciting. I feel privileged to have been able to record their growth, both as quiltmakers and as individuals, and have found their stories enthralling. The energy with which many of them approach their work is almost overwhelming, and their striving for excellence is truly inspiring. Each makes wonderful quilts, reflecting one of the traditions of quiltmaking. While some are professional quiltmakers, others quilt for their own pleasure. As you read about their journeys and absorb the details of how they work, remember that each one started by simply learning the basic traditional skills of quiltmaking. The constant quest for exemplary workmanship and the ability to grasp every opportunity has enabled them to become the leading exponents of traditional quiltmaking in Australia.

CIRCLES OF THE PAST

185 cm x 201 cm , 1993

1850s remembered

JUDY DAY

ANDREW PAYNE

'Do you know how to do "Cathedral Window"?' This question, asked innocently enough by her mother, sent Judy Day on an adventure into quiltmaking that continues to this day. Judy copied the appropriate sheets from her collection of craft books to give to her mother, then decided to try her hand at a 'Cathedral Window' block herself. Although she finally completed enough sections for a cushion cover, she didn't enjoy the process, finding it complicated and restricting.

Quilts on display in a fabric shop in Sydney were Judy's only other exposure to patchwork and did little to encourage her to investigate the craft any further: 'They were made of squares all the same size and I thought they looked very repetitive. I decided that I would never want to do that sort of work.'

As a child, surrounded by creativity, Judy was encouraged to sew by her mother, an expert needlewoman and dressmaker. In fact, when the new electric sewing machine arrived in the house, Judy, aged five, was the first to try it out. Even before starting school, she was able to knit and crochet, skills taught to her by her grandmother. Her father, a doctor and keen photographer, also encouraged her artistic endeavours.

Following her initial foray into patchwork with the 'Cathedral Window', Judy wanted to see if there was more to patchwork than she had so far experienced. While on holidays in 1987, she purchased a book on sampler quilts and found herself scouring the local shop for supplies. She had several blocks under construction even before returning home:

This was much more exciting than 'Cathedral Window' or just squares. I simply traced the shapes onto writing paper, the only paper I had on hand, and made a paper pattern just like in dressmaking. Then I pinned it onto the fabric, matching the grain line carefully, and cut out the shape. I sewed the seams, eyeballing the seam allowance.

Judy had worked out her own completely unique system which she still uses today. 'If I am sewing someone else's blocks and the seam line is marked in pencil, the pencil line really throws me,' explains Judy. She returned from that holiday determined to complete the blocks and do more patchwork.

Still working from books and magazine articles, Judy made several traditional quilts, using simple block designs, including a house quilt in primary colours for her daughter Margot. Next, she investigated Log Cabin quilts, cutting the one-and-a-half-inch strips carefully along the grain with her small pair of scissors. The grain line of the fabric is still very important to Judy. If there is a fabric that has been printed off-grain, then she will cut along the grain line rather than follow the fabric pattern!

Having worked from books for some time, Judy was quite astounded by the first quilt show she attended in 1987.

I had never seen anything like it. The books I had been reading didn't prepare me for the variety of work on show. It was far beyond anything I had imagined, especially the contemporary work. I was surprised that there were few really traditional quilts. I had expected to be able to have a close look at the sorts of quilts I had been reading about.

Judy joined The Quilters' Guild and a local Sydney group, the St Ives Quilters, which provided her with friends who shared her growing passion for quiltmaking.

Interest in Baltimore quilts was growing in the quilting community and the first of the publications documenting these wonderful quilts, by Elly Sienkiewicz, caught Judy's eye. Using the book, Judy taught herself needleturn appliqué:

I wasn't keen on the freezer paper; it seemed to get in the way when I was turning the seam allowance under. I like to draw the design on the background with a water-soluble blue pen, and lay the pieces on the background, then I turn under the seam allowance, following the guide on the background fabric.

Judy prefers not to draw on the appliqué pieces themselves, unless they are very complex. For her small quilt, 'Whirling Feathers', entered in the 1994 Quilt Show in Sydney, she had to make thirty-two feathers. Because of the difficulty of the design she had chosen, Judy drew the pattern onto the freezer paper, cut it out, then ironed it onto the red fabric. Next, she drew around the shape with a fine black pen and removed the freezer paper. The black ink line on the appliqué pieces was turned under and hidden during the appliqué process.

Judy only marks small sections of her quilt at a time with blue marking pen, and sponges the marks out as soon as she finishes each section. She is careful to rinse the entire quilt, when it is completed, to make sure all the chemicals from the marking pen are removed from the fabric.

Judy next turned her attentions to the techniques of needleturn appliqué to create her own variations on the traditional Baltimore patterns. Judy took nine months to assemble her first appliqué quilt, 'Beyond Baltimore'. The quilting took a further three years! 'Beyond Baltimore' took out two awards in the 1992 Quilt Show: second place in the Amateur Appliqué section and The Noreen Dunn Memorial Award for Excellence in Quilting:

BEYOND BALTIMORE, *201 cm x 207 cm, 1993*

TERRENCE DARCY

ANDREW EITON

ANDREW PAYNE

I felt completely overwhelmed — especially when I was awarded the quilting prize. I have never been shown how to quilt and feel I get there, but very slowly. I have just looked at books and watched how others quilt. So this was a tremendous thrill.

Judy's excellence in appliqué had been already noticed. She was the proud winner of a Bernina sewing machine as her block 'Bird in a Wreath' was chosen as the best traditional block in a national competition in 1990. To add to the excitement of winning, the news arrived on her birthday!

Coupled with Judy's continuing love of appliqué was a growing interest in antique quilts made in Britain during the last century, particularly the medallion quilts. Judy was overwhelmed with the quilts she saw at the Victoria and Albert Museum in London. Although there are not many quilts on public display, Judy had made arrangements to see twenty-five of the quilts made during the last century and kept in storage. One of the quilts used the 'Steeplechase' block, surrounding

a printed panel. Judy took up the challenge to replicate this quilt, choosing an appliquéd panel for the centre of the quilt, rather than a printed panel:

Although I realise the quilt is not an original design, I enjoyed the challenge of achieving the same look. It is important to find just the right fabric for each shape. I look for designs that emulate the old fabrics. A lot of them had very small prints and it

is hardest to find the lighter fabrics. It is only that I have quite a collection that I was able to find what I wanted for the quilt.

This quilt, 'Circles of the Past', was awarded equal first prize in the 1993 Quilt Show.

Many of Judy's fabrics are samples sent from quilt shops all over the country. She puts them all in a large bag and gets great pleasure from hunting through the small pieces, looking for just the right fabric. For her quilt, 'Just Leaves', inspired by a 1930s quilt 'Autumn Leaves', which won the Chicago World Fair, Judy required one hundred and fifty different green fabrics for the leaves. They were all found in this seemingly bottomless bag of five-centimetre sample squares. 'Just Leaves', was one of the traditional quilts selected for The Colours of Australia exhibition which will tour Australia for five years between 1995 and 2000.

For her award-winning appliqué, Judy uses a blind stitch, working from right to left with the appliqué piece towards her. This gives a very neat finish: 'I feel that you can't get the stitches hidden with slipstitch. My stitches are really close together with only about a millimetre between them.'

The challenge to have a quilt in The Quilt Show each year provides Judy with the impetus to improve her work and sets a deadline for finishing each piece:

I am a perfectionist and try to improve my techniques all the time. If I'm not satisfied with the workmanship, I'll unpick it. I would be thrilled if my work provided inspiration to others.

Her appetite whetted, Judy is keen to investigate further the English-style medallion quilts. One quilt that has particularly enthralled her is a medallion quilt with an appliqué centre, surrounded by hundreds of tiny squares, all sewn over papers:

My ambition is to make this quilt, but I won't be doing it over papers. I love the colourings, typical of nineteenth-century English patchwork, with many shades of brown. My collection of fabrics is growing, with swatches pasted in an exercise book for future reference. I'm looking forward to the challenge.

Judy feels it is important that traditional work continues, and does not diminish: 'Australian quiltmakers have achieved so much in such a short time. There is now more of a balance between traditional and contemporary work in the shows and this is wonderful to see.'

Having spent many years being involved in numerous crafts, Judy is now content with quiltmaking: 'I do it because I love it.'

OAK LEAF AND REEL (*top left*), 28.5 cm square, 1994
1800 REVISITED (*left*), 123 cm square, 1992
WHIRLING FEATHERS (*below*), 101 cm square, 1994

STUART HAY

FLORIADE

250 cm x 275 cm, 1989

Awash with colour

JUDY TURNER

ANDREW PAYNE

Postage stamp quilts have always intrigued and delighted those who appreciate the process of quiltmaking. Thousands of tiny pieces, often no bigger than a postage stamp, are sewn together to create wonderful quilts that still speak to us of the quiltmaker's dedication and determination. Men, too, have been captured by the challenge to create wonderful quilts using very small pieces. Their vibrant patchwork tablecloths and quilts, made from scraps of woollen soldiers' uniforms, are part of the Australian quilt heritage.

Judy Turner, with her many-pieced quilts, has captured something of this tradition and welcomes it into the twentieth century in her unique style, awash with a flurry of bright and glorious colours.

From very early in her quiltmaking history, Judy was attracted to quilts using a myriad of fabrics, shading from dark to light. A quilt designed by Grace Earl and featured in *Quilting – Patchwork and Applique* (Sunset Books, 1981), provided the catalyst for Judy's first non-traditional quilt, 'Ashes of Roses'. First, Judy set about collecting as many shades of pink fabrics as she could and was able to find over sixty prints suitable for her project – a fairly remarkable feat in 1983.

At the same time, Judy had seen the film *Quilts in Women's Lives* and was taken by the use of a felt wallboard by one of the quilters in the film. In no time at all, Ian, her very supportive husband, had built one in their bedroom, giving Judy the freedom to position and move her many pink triangles as she wished.

Always an enthusiastic stitcher, having learned to sew from her talented mother, Judy took patchwork and quilting classes with Margaret Rolfe and Wendy Saclier in Canberra in 1981. Working conditions were fairly cramped, with twenty students in Margaret's lounge room, but this didn't seem to dampen anyone's enthusiasm – certainly not Judy's. She had made nine traditional quilts before experimenting with 'Ashes of Roses'.

Unable to buy cotton fabrics during winter in Canberra, the collection of light and dark pink fabrics became the inspiration and material for Judy's next two quilts. She experimented with strips cut from the fabrics she had on hand, cutting more than was needed, and created 'Daybreak Island', her first pictorial quilt.

The difficulty of obtaining a good range of fabrics in the 1980s made Judy look beyond her home city, seeking mail order fabric samples from all over the

JONATHON CHESTER

SEVENTY-TWO TRAIL ST, *198 cm x 143 cm, 1991*

Show in 1986 voted it the winner of the Viewers' Choice prize.

The move to using very strong and multicoloured fabrics came when Judy's mother became seriously ill.

I wanted to capture my mother's excitement and enthusiasm about flowers and colour, to use the rich fabrics I had collected for over a year to somehow represent her wonderful garden and her creativity. My quilt, 'Floriade', was very special to the family and, because of the emotional turmoil in our lives, proved very difficult to make. In the end, I think the quilt does justice to the memory of my mother.

The collection of fabrics for 'Floriade' started with one fabric that Judy really loved and grew as she gathered every other fabric she could find with colours from the original one. Two types of shading have been used in the quilt. The strips on each square are shaded, with quilt-as-you-go techniques employed to attach each strip. The completed squares are arranged in a pleasing wash of colour from dark to light with the large florals in the centre of the quilt. Seams on both front and back are covered with a floral strip.

Completely captivated by the effect of shading her fabrics, Judy planned to make a wall quilt, using small squares to create the wash of colour for the background. Originally planning to feature a wreath of flowers in the centre, with the colourwash as a backdrop, Judy found herself adding a pieced fence and

country. These samples were then left in the letterbox for her friends to look at and order if they wished.

One of these sample fabrics inspired Judy to design a five-petalled flower which formed the centre of the medallion quilt 'Beyond the Trellis': 'This was the first time I used shading of fabrics in the border of a quilt. I also tried to use my quilting to a greater advantage, designing a motif that echoed the flower shape in the centre. The quilting lines crossed over the piecing, blending the colours.' The visitors to The Sydney Quilt

large flowers. The shapes were cut from printed fabric and hand-appliquéd to the fence:

I am intrigued by the effect of the subconscious on my work. In the course of the quilters' master class in Sydney in 1991, I came to the realisation that my mother's memories of my brother and me, climbing a fence at our old home in Trail Street were depicted in this quilt. This memory had made my mother very happy, and she had shared that joy with us. I had unconsciously captured this image in my quilt, 'Seventy-two Trail St'.

The myriad pieces that make up 'Colourwash Cascade' are set in a post-and-rail design. Starting with very tiny pieces, Judy made what was destined to be a class sample. Unhappy with the result, she discarded it as too difficult for a class and ended up working with

BICA PHOTOGRAPHICS

COLOURWASH CASCADE *(left)*, 263 cm x 182 cm, 1992
ASHES OF ROSES *(above)*, 140 cm x 226 cm, 1983

MICHAEL PUGH

much larger strips: 'The larger pieces were a challenge, but once I began working with them, I felt the result was very successful. Even the discarded section fitted beautifully into the centre of the quilt with a second matching piece.' The small pieces seem to cascade over the edges of the central squares because of the cleverly placed tones. This quilt was awarded equal first prize in the theme section at the Quilt Show in Sydney in 1993.

As a result of one of her early quilts, 'Daybreak Island', being seen by some Tasmanian quilters, Judy was invited by the Bellerive Community Arts Centre in Hobart to be the 1993 artist in residence to complete a wall quilt. Working with a group of members, Judy was asked to interpret in fabric a beautiful photograph of

ANDREW PAYNE

Kangaroo Bay, with the familiar bulk of Mount Wellington in the background. The design of the completed quilt picks up the gold and pink of the sunset, reflected in the shimmering waters of the river:

I was thrilled to be asked to direct this exciting project. Working with women who were not necessarily quilters was quite a challenge, but the finished quilt showed how much everyone had learned about technique as well as colour and design.

Since 1982, teaching has also been an important outlet for Judy, but as her priority was always to be at home for her family, lessons were conducted in her home after the children were in bed: 'I have always wanted more than just a clean house, and patchwork has provided me with the opportunity to express my creativity'. Now Judy is a highly sought-after tutor and travels widely each year, sharing her skills in a variety of workshops based on her wonderful quilts, as well as conducting a full teaching program at her home.

The most popular workshop is Colourwash Nine Patch which Judy has taught over fifty times:

Many people tell me they like the way I use colour and the way I put colours together. The important thing for me is colour value, that is whether a fabric is light, medium or dark. I use a traditional block to show my students how you can change the shapes in the block when you change the colour values. I also like to demonstrate what can happen when you blend colours the way I do. In the colourwash workshop, every student has approximately fifty-four fabrics. I like to check each person's fabrics and everyone watches me rearrange them, if necessary. That way everyone learns about colour value.

After these electric sessions with fabric and colour value, Judy's students claim they are much braver with fabric choices, understand a lot more about colour value and will never look at fabrics in the same way again.

The inspiration for Judy's own work often comes from a wonderful image she has seen in her library of picture books, perhaps of a vase of flowers or a garden scene:

It will be the colour combinations that attract me and I'll search through my fabrics and collect those colour combinations, ranging from light to dark. When I look at the collection of fabrics, I can see only the tone of the fabric and can easily pick out gaps in the run from

light to dark. Only then will I buy a new fabric to fill the gap. I always like to include one fabric as a real 'lifter' to the other fabrics, and often find ochre a very useful addition.

Judy continues to explore new ways of using her multicoloured palette of fabrics. Her family provides great support and encouragement. In return, Judy has assembled for her family a portfolio of her work, with thoughts and inspirations, clippings and cuttings, brochures and catalogues scattered among photographs of her quilts, creating an invaluable and greatly treasured record of her work.

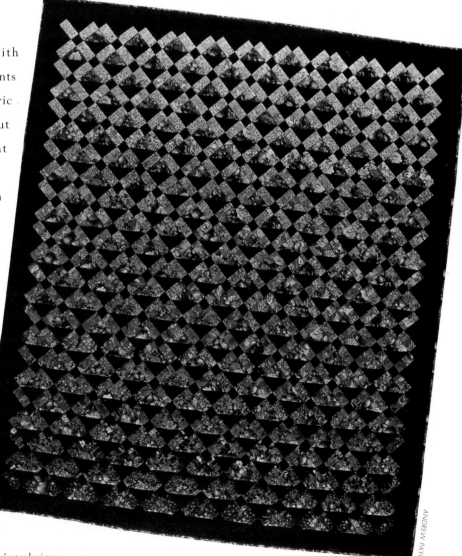

WORK IN PROGRESS *(far left) showing Judy's technique*
BLACK JEWEL *(above), 234 cm x 206 cm, 1994*

ROGER DECKER

AUSTRALIANA VICTORIANA

70 cm x 110 cm, 1988

Crazy about quilts

WENDY SACLIER

ANDREW PAYNE

McKinlay, in north-west Queensland, is a tiny township, surrounded by red dust and saltbush, an image of a harsh almost desperate lifestyle. Sketching, stitching and other genteel pursuits seem out of place in such an environment. Wendy Saclier's memories of her childhood in McKinlay are far from harsh and dreary:

I have the loveliest memories of mother doing wonderful embroidery. She especially loved to embroider flowers, as she was a keen gardener. I was taught to embroider and learned to treasure every bit of fabric and thread. With the post arriving only once a week, and everything having to come from Townsville, in northern Queensland, what arrived was very precious. Nothing was thrown away.

From an early age, Wendy was encouraged to conserve and make do. Her grandmother's verandah housed stretchers for itinerant workers which were covered with kangaroo skin rugs, patchworked and edged with felt. Cheesecloth and carded wool formed the basis for the makeshift quilts in Wendy's home, made in two or three colours and quilted in simple rectangles.

The year 1976 found Wendy living in Canberra. Her neighbour, Judy Thompson had spent a year in Washington where she had seen and enjoyed quilts. She encouraged Wendy to visit a patchwork display by Margaret Rolfe, now a well-known international author of patchwork books, who had recently returned to Australia after a visit to the United States:

I remember how excited we all were. From then on, meetings were held regularly and every snippet of information from magazines was cut out and saved, and we pored over every book we could find.

Wendy's first quilt was appliquéd, followed by several excursions into patchwork clothing, including a patchwork skirt in bright yellow, blue and red (which Wendy hopes will never see the light of day again) and a collection of blue and brown quilts, using traditional blocks.

As the Canberra group grew, there was a demand for classes. Margaret Rolfe and Wendy organised these for several years. From these early beginnings came the Canberra Quilters, the first quilters' guild in Australia. Many well-known quiltmakers in Australia today can trace their initial introduction to quiltmaking to those early classes.

Circumstances often encourage new directions. Wendy was given a bag of scraps of exotic fabrics at the time she was becoming concerned for her mother, Vivienne, who she felt had too much time on her hands. Remembering her childhood lesson and not wanting to throw anything out, Wendy decided to make a crazy patchwork quilt, using the fabrics she had been given, and encouraged her mother to work the embroidery on the patched squares:

It was a very happy decision. Mum and I have developed a whole new dimension to our relationship. We respond to each other and really enjoy what the other person does. The satin stitch, grub roses and buttonhole work is done by Mum, together with any appliqué work needed, and I do the basic piecing. When the embroidered blocks come back to me, I do the seam-line embroidery and beading. I also love to experiment with the traditional stitches, combining stitches, adding French knots in groups of twos or threes and constantly coming up with new effects. That first crazy patch quilt has an almost naive charm. The pieces were much larger than those I use now, and Mum's stitching is now more refined and varied. In the true tradition of crazy patchwork, the quilt contains memories of each member of the family.

Wendy and her mother, Vivienne, standing in front of 'Crazy Garden'

The unstructured form of crazy patchwork suits Wendy very well, as she describes herself as a non-mathematician who is not very exact. She enjoys the freedom that working with textiles in this way – with no measuring required – gives her.

The pieces are applied to sheeting or old shirts – preferably something that has been used – to give softness to the quilt. Placement of the pieces is by trial and error:

Just throw down a few fabrics and stand back to decide what you think. The important thing is to keep going; everything changes when the embellishments go on. The pieces become smaller and the colours you use take up the strength of colour of the embellishments. If there is one colour used systematically in each block then that will provide the unifying factor for the whole background. I always try to get a balance in the shapes and avoid any large blobs of colour. To achieve this, I try to use colours that blend rather than contrast, so that no colour jumps out at you. If I'm not happy with a piece, I can always cover it up with an embellishment. That is the beauty of crazy patchwork.

Wendy's classes are generally composed of people who have done patchwork before. Wendy encourages her students to use a single-colour theme, if they feel unsure using multicoloured fabrics, and to keep the applied pieces approximately the same size.

She feels that crazy patchwork helps quilters to make the step into unstructured work from the very strongly structured constraints of traditional patchwork: 'Some people make this transition quite happily, others want to put everything as it will be when finished. This simply isn't possible as everything changes when the pieces are sewn onto the foundation.'

Wendy is currently working on a strongly coloured quilt, endeavouring to capture the concept of time and the way colour changes during the day. The pieces 'move through the day' encapsulating each mood and each shadow. Each small block is pinned up on Wendy's 'favourite-ideas wall' and careful consideration is given to its placement. The size of the work is not predetermined. When the concept has been captured, then she will consider the piece to be finished.

Wendy is also working on a small nine-patch quilt for a friend's fiftieth birthday. The piece is on the wall board, awaiting last-minute embellishments. Each block represents some aspect of her friend's life, including her love of cats and knitting.

The traditional crazy patchwork quilts, recorded in Penny McMorris's book, *Crazy Quilts,* are a constant source of inspiration for Wendy, who particularly admires the quilts showing symmetrical work and the charm quilts. In her classes, Wendy likes to share these wonderful historic quilts with her students, maintaining that connecting thread with the quiltmakers of the past. Some of the fabrics are unobtainable today, the richness of texture or colour, particularly gold, is impossible to replicate. Judith Montano's work is also a source of inspiration, with pictorial scenes embellished with traditional crazy patchwork stitches. Her work provides yet another path along which

BLOOM ON – FIFTY ROSES FOR FIFTY YEARS *(above right), 17 cm square, 1985* Wendy's first crazy patchwork quilt *(right),* 136 cm square, 1980

ANDREW PAYNE

ANDREW PAYNE

CATTY FANNIT, *94 cm x 120 cm, 1992*

ANDREW PAYNE

It was like Christmas when a finished block arrived, and I would pore over it to see just what Mum had done. Only then would I add the embroidery along the seam lines, using stranded embroidery thread, then add beads and other embellishments. I really like adding the spiders and frogs.

So highly regarded is Wendy's work that a cot quilt made by her is part of the Legislative Assembly Collection in Canberra, ACT, while a crazy patchwork tea cosy forms part of the Lismore Embroiderers Guild's permanent collection. Her quilt 'Australiana Victoriana' is part of the Quilters' Guild's collection Quilts Covering Australia. Wendy was also invited to participate in an international tour of Australian quilts, organised by Jan Irvine for the Department of Foreign Affairs and Trade in 1991 and, most recently, was a member of the ACT Cultural Council, a government body appointed to investigate and distribute funds to the arts and crafts programmes.

In her teaching role, Wendy has the opportunity to see the creativity of many of her students blossom, and enjoys passing on her skills. She is aware of the huge change in the way people are approaching their quiltmaking, at the same time recognising that traditions will always have an important role in providing the basis for creativity. As Wendy says: 'In Australia we have a great diversity of influences, not

Wendy is quite happy for her students to travel.

Occasionally, Wendy takes out one of her most outstanding works, 'Crazy Garden', and adds a few extra embellishments to its surface. Using her extensive collection of cream fabrics, Wendy pieced the blocks for this quilt and sent them to her mother who was living in Ulladulla on the far south coast of New South Wales. Here, Vivienne had established an exquisite garden and this love of the garden is reflected in the extensive embroidery on the quilt. Flowers and creatures abound, providing an endless feast of beauty. The quilt took eight months to complete, with the blocks being sent to and fro:

only the colours around us and where we live, but the broad spectrum of multicultural traditions. This has resulted in a fantastic explosion in quiltmaking.'

Wendy is content with crazy patchwork, with the occasional experimentation in fabric collages, and delights in making lovely gifts for her friends.

Quiltmaking provides the balance in her life; it is the calming, relaxing element in an otherwise hectic schedule as a speech therapist at a busy clinic: 'It provides the outlet for creativity, an expression of colour, of how you feel about the world around you and what you love – and the other lovely thing for me is that it is shared with my mother.'

CHRISTMAS CRAZY (right), 60 cm square, 1992
Wendy adding finishing touches to 'Crazy Garden' (below)

ANDREW PAYNE

27

ANDREW PAYNE

RING AROUND ROSIE

45 cm x 65 cm, 1990

Chintz cutouts

MARJORIE PATTERSON

Of an academic bent at school, Marjorie ignored her mother's entreaties to teach her to sew. 'It's sad to think of the things I didn't learn from her,' laments Marjorie. 'She embroidered beautifully and made everything for me. I still have some of the duchesse sets, which are real treasures.'

With a career in the medical arena as her goal, Marjorie continued her academic pursuits and became an occupational therapist. Along with physiology and anatomy lectures, and work in hospitals, came hands-on experience of fifty-two widely varied crafts. Having never done any handwork before, Marjorie discovered that she loved it all:

We learned the usual skills of spinning and weaving, basket-making, knitting and embroidery, together with such amazing crafts as fly-tying, and Austrian cane-weaving for chairs. My favourite was weaving, I had my own four-shaft loom, weaving my own fine tweeds.

Eventually, Marjorie and her husband, Alan, were to own a small rural property in Robertson, in the Southern Highlands of New South Wales where they sheared their own sheep. Marjorie gave all the sheep individual names, and enjoyed spinning and weaving their wool:

There was no craft movement in the 1950s and 1960s, just the Embroiderer's Guild and the Spinners and Weavers. The influence of the Red Cross was still strong. I joined the Embroiderer's Guild as, much to my surprise, I began to really enjoy embroidery.

Marjorie also became a founding member of the North Shore Crafts Cooperative in Sydney, selling both her weaving and copper enamelling, another craft which she embraced with great enthusiasm.

Ready to try anything, Marjorie became a partner in The Crewel Goblin, a Danish embroidery supply shop. It was there that she met a fellow embroiderer, Trudy Billingsley, now an internationally known textile artist. Trudy introduced Marjorie to patchwork and quilting and agreed to give lessons at the shop:

Those first lessons were wonderful and filled my mind with all sorts of ideas. Patchwork is great for getting the creative juices going. My aqua and navy sampler quilt completed in the class is still treasured, even though I am very aware of all the mistakes.

Bit by bit, Marjorie's embroidery took second place as patchwork took over, so much so that Marjorie became part of the steering committee responsible for the establishment of The Quilters' Guild in New South Wales. The concept of forming a guild for quilters, similar to the Embroiderer's Guild, appealed to Marjorie. She was eager to duplicate for quilters the enjoyment, interaction and inspiration that she had found among embroiderers.

Marjorie continued to extend her own skills by learning to draft her own patterns with the assistance of her architect husband, Alan. This provided yet another dimension to her quiltmaking, one she really enjoyed. Initially she didn't make anything she didn't have a picture for, but classes with Virginia Avery and Joan Schultz changed all that. As part of its education programme, The Quilters' Guild invited these two American quiltmakers to Australia. They were both instrumental in providing a broader base for Marjorie's work. Ideas on incorporating patchwork in clothing were explored with Virginia, and original design work using reflections and rotations was investigated with Joan. Marjorie continues to work with both these aspects of quiltmaking, while preserving the traditional aspects of her work. 'Alan says I have a graph-paper mind', muses

ANDREW PAYNE

RING OF FLOWERS, *15 cm x 18 cm, 1988*

Marjorie. 'Everything I do, whether it is weaving, cross-stitch, bobbin lace or patchwork, is on a grid. I guess I like the symmetry.'

With her interest in clothing stimulated by Virginia Avery, Marjorie experimented with garments which incorporated many of the traditional skills she had refined. While favouring symmetry in quiltmaking, Marjorie opted for asymmetry when it came to making jackets and vests. She wore one of her appliquéd vests to The Quilt Market in Houston, Texas in 1985. The vest, appliquéd in the traditional way with a large poppy design, made such an impact that she was invited to participate in the Concord Fashion Show, a first for any Australian. A little overawed by such an honour, Marjorie's creative talents worked overtime. She discovered a wonderful fabric full of vibrant roses and it became the inspiration for the design she was preparing for the show, prompting her to investigate broderie perse as a technique for applying the roses. While wanting to use exciting fabrics as the basis for appliqué, Marjorie broke from the traditional method of attaching the cut-out roses to the background with buttonhole stitch. She preferred to cut a seam allowance around each shape and turn the seam allowance under:

This way, I can get a look that suggests the pieces have been slightly stuffed. The effect is even more pronounced when the shapes are very tiny. And, of course, when you work this way nobody knows where the flower really ends, only you.

Since that first highly successful experiment with broderie perse, Marjorie has maintained a continual love of chintz cut-outs, made famous during the Victorian era when it was essential to use these ornate and costly fabrics sparingly.

Following that initial class with Trudy Billingsley, Marjorie has continually taught patchwork classes and promoted the craft in whatever capacity she could. In 1985, she found herself teaching patchwork to American women on a P&O Cruise:

ANDREW PAYNE

Vest decorated with broderie perse (above), 1993
BUTTERFLIES IN MY GARDEN *(below), 35 cm square, 1994*

They just loved it, and couldn't wait to see what I was going to teach them each day. I had to make up all the small projects, as there were no reference books or magazines then. With only fifty dollars to buy all the materials and requirements, I had to be very inventive but I really had a wonderful time. My fee was passage paid to Vanuatu for Alan and myself, with accommodation in the bowels of the vessel with the crew.

Always willing to take up a new challenge, Marjorie met with Barbara Meredith and a group of friends in Armidale in 1987 to discuss the first Australasian Patchwork and Quilting Symposium. This was an

ambitious proposal to bring quiltmakers from every state in Australia for five days of workshops and lectures, given by both American and Australian tutors. The venture was a resounding success and Marjorie participated for three years, enjoying, as always, the creativity generated when a group of craftspeople get together.

During an extended stay on Norfolk Island, for which she was only allowed to pack minimal quilting supplies, Marjorie turned her hand to making miniature quilts, incorporating broderie perse. The delightful result, 'Ring of Flowers', with the tiniest flowers applied in a wreath, set Marjorie on a

ANDREW PAYNE

new path in her quiltmaking – creating an image using a traditional technique to apply her miniature cut-outs.

Most recently, Marjorie has combined her skills for miniature broderie perse with Alan's skills as a painter. Inspired by a workshop which involved piecing a house block, then decorating it with embroidery, Marjorie asked Alan to paint a suitable scene on calico. She then used broderie perse flowers, combined with embroidered leaves and stems, to provide an extra dimension to the painted scenes. 'Alan and I really love to work together. There is no sense of competition between us, at all,' Marjorie says. 'We have a great admiration for each other's work and are a wonderful happy combination.'

For this very fine work, Marjorie uses Serafil, a thread generally used for overlocking and the finest crewel needles she can find. With a basket of her favourite floral fabric at her feet, and a box of embroidery threads of all shades close at hand, Marjorie chooses each flower individually, and cuts it out with fine scissors, leaving approximately four millimetres seam allowance. Holding the flower with her long thumbnail (an essential according to Marjorie), she works from right to left so that the thumb can continue to hold the flower in the right position, while she tucks the seam allowance under with the needle. Marjorie's classes in which she teaches this technique have proved very popular, but Alan isn't so sure of its merit as he is

GARDEN CORNER, *20 cm x 25 cm, 1994*
This is the first of Marjorie and Alan's joint projects

required to paint the background for each workshop participant!

Each year brings new challenges and new opportunities for Marjorie. She continues to teach each week, as well as running workshops for the local church women. This group of industrious ladies made quilts for Triple Care Farm, where young people affected by drugs are given an opportunity to rebuild their lives while working and studying in a sheltered environment. Marjorie also belongs to Kiama Quilters on the South Coast of New South Wales, and to SQUAWs (Southern Quilters at Work), which is a group of fairly advanced quilters who meet to share and encourage each other. Many local groups enjoy attending Marjorie's workshops, as do groups from all over the country. Marjorie's enthusiasm and encouragement is infectious:

There is enormous variation in quiltmaking. It can be fine work or quite rough and still have enormous appeal. It's not as hard on the eyes as crewel or cross-stitch embroidery, but still promotes that desire for accuracy. Quiltmaking gives everyone an opportunity to explore their own creativity and to play with colour, design and texture.

Marjorie boasts that she'll go anywhere and do anything. In 1994, she travelled to Broken Hill in the far west of New South Wales as part of the Country Workshops programme of The Quilters' Guild:

I have had to slow down a little after my by-pass surgery. I have a strong faith, and I had to look at my priorities and go in a different direction. Now my faith means a lot more to me, and my family are all-important. I am still too busy but I try and pace myself. I do hope, however, that the future brings more quilting and more people into my life.

All the bits and pieces Marjorie gathers before beginning a new picture (above left)
Marjorie's hands at work (left)

MIDNIGHT MAGIC

197 cm x 245 cm, 1992

Gridded to perfection

KERRILYN GAVIN

ANDREW PAYNE

From very early in her quiltmaking career, Kerrilyn has been attracted to grids. One of her earliest quilts, an aqua Dresden Plate which Kerrilyn treasures and has on her bed, features a large grid on the border and a smaller grid in the large centre of each plate. Looking at it now, she feels it is under-quilted, but in 1984 she was quite impressed with the amount of quilting she had used. The impact of using grids as part of the quilting design was established and Kerrilyn has continued to use this technique in many of her award-winning quilts:

When I draw a grid on a plain piece of fabric, I am making my own fabric, creating a sculptured backdrop for my quilting design. Always in the back of my mind, as I am designing, is the thought that the quilting will stand out beautifully, when I have a grid behind it.

There were always sewing machines available for Kerrilyn and her five sisters to experiment with while they were growing up. All the girls learned sewing at school and made clothes for themselves.

For Kerrilyn, quilt-making began in 1983 in Canberra:

I didn't ever want to make a traditional sampler quilt, so I learned the basic skills by making a quilt using the Sailboat block. After making the Dresden Plate quilt, I found I was attracted to the quilting process. It was something I thoroughly enjoyed doing.

In anticipation of the Bicentennial Quilt Show, Kerrilyn designed and executed 'Heirloom of Wildflowers'. Always looking for interesting features in her quilts, Kerrilyn chose to outline the motifs with embroidered back stitch, providing the only colour on the quilt. Using elements from several sources, Kerrilyn designed the various floral emblems for each state, while the central oval contained the national emblem, the wattle, with its two hundred blossoms representing the Bicentennial.

A 1990 visit to the annual American Quilters Society Quilt Show in Paducah, Kentucky, convinced Kerrilyn that Australian quilters could compete favourably with their American counterparts. She

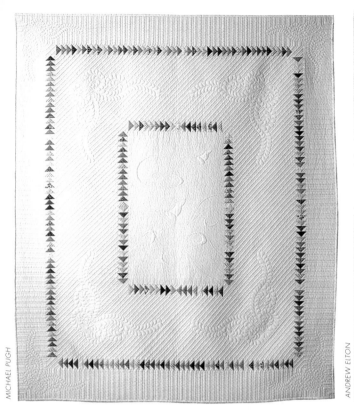

FLIGHT OF FORTY (*above*), *230 cm x 197 cm, 1991*
ON THE WINGS OF FREEDOM (*right*), *200 cm x 240 cm, 1994*

submitted 'Flight of Forty' for judging in the 1991 exhibition and received an Honourable Mention in the Other Techniques category. The quilt had already won Viewers' Choice in the Sydney Show in 1990 and second place in the Traditional Pieced category. Encouraged by her success, she submitted 'Midnight Magic' to the 1992 Paducah show. Moving away from the white background, Kerrilyn achieved a spectacular result by using black and red as her colour scheme for this quilt, which was completed over a two-year period. The Celtic designs are her own and some she adapted from Philomena Whycheck's book on Celtic quilts.

As always Kerrilyn's design is gridded, creating a wonderful backdrop to the individual designs: 'I don't like to copy. I always prefer to do my own thing. While I don't see myself as an artist, I have some artistic flair and so I always want to put my own interpretation into my designs.'

Bill Schroeder from the American Quilting Museum

was so impressed with the quilt that he invited Kerrilyn to donate it to the museum. While declining the offer, Kerrilyn was extremely flattered that her work had gained such recognition.

Often Kerrilyn spends several years planning a quilt. Her entry into the Inaugural Melbourne Quilt Show in 1992 'On Wings of Freedom' was two years in the planning. More than three years before she started making the quilt, she had jotted down the idea for a quilt that represented a flight of butterflies:

Funnily enough, it was only when I was right in the process of making the quilt I realised where the inspiration had come from. When I was young, we had a large verandah around the house. The grapevines entwined on the verandah were a haven for butterflies, and I would sit and watch them for hours. All these elements are in my quilt.

The leaf fabric Kerrilyn had bought while visiting the United States became the starting point for the quilt, providing the leaves of the grapevine: 'I often get

HEIRLOOM OF WILDFLOWERS *(right)*, *210 cm x 230 cm, 1988*
Detail of Heirloom of Wildflowers

inspiration from fabric and know exactly what I will do with it,' says Kerrilyn. 'Although I don't see myself as a fabricaholic, I will buy three or four metres of a particular fabric if it 'speaks' to me.' The template for the quilting pattern was an actual grape leaf.

'On Wings of Freedom' was sent to Paducah in 1993 and was awarded third place in the Other Techniques category.

One corner of Kerrilyn's studio is covered with ribbons and awards she has received for her quiltmaking. Kerrilyn is reluctant to put them on more prominent display as she is very modest about her work. The standard of excellence she has reached with her quiltmaking provides Kerrilyn with a deep sense of personal satisfaction.

Kerrilyn enjoys working with just two fabrics. Her current work in progress, 'Music from the Heart', uses only two: a white background fabric, purchased in the USA, and a red print for the hearts. Once the design had been decided, Kerrilyn prepared templates for the heart appliqué. Having marked the wrong side of the fabric with pencil, she machine-sews along the lines, providing a sharp turning edge for the appliqué. The seam allowance is then turned under and basted, giving Kerrilyn a crisp edge for appliquéing to the background fabric. Each piece is pinned in place before it is appliquéd, as are paper cut-out shapes of the proposed quilting pattern. Kerrilyn gives much consideration to the placement of the quilting pattern, ensuring a perfect balance with the coloured appliqué.

On the hearts quilt, she has designed a quilting pattern which employs a stylised musical score, featuring musical notes made from hearts. She draws one-sixteenth of the full-sized pattern, then transfers it to the background fabric, a procedure that requires considerable care as the pattern needs to be reversed in

37

Kerrilyn is working on the design of Music from the Heart

ANDREW PAYNE

That first line is critical when drawing up a grid. If I get the first line correct, then I can measure out from it. The easiest way to get an accurate line is to fold the fabric carefully from corner to corner, and finger-press it. Then I am off and running. If I am using a rectangular grid, I fold the quilt top in half and work from there. Every single mark from then

on is important. I measure out carefully from the fold line, marking with a dot. Then the dots are joined. I like to work on a fully extended table tennis table to mark up my grid. It is not important to have the grid lines meeting critical points in the design. When it is all quilted, the grid simply appears as a background to the design.

some sections. Kerrilyn completes this process on the wallboard, using a pencil. Once the quilting pattern is transferred and the appliqué pieces are pinned in place, Kerrilyn is ready to remove the quilt top from the wallboard and complete the appliqué. Next, Kerrilyn decided to outline each of the heart notes in red to provide a balance of colour to the wreath of red in the centre. Then she adds the grid lines, with a separation determined by the motifs in the appliqué and quilting design. As the appliqué hearts are quite small in her present project, Kerrilyn has decided to use a one-and-a-half-centimetre grid:

Once the grid is marked on the quilt top, Kerrilyn can get down to the serious business of quilting, often working eight to ten hours a day to complete a piece for a show.

Quiltskills 1993, a series of workshops held in conjunction with The Sydney Quilt Festival, provided

Kerrilyn's first opportunity to pass on her skills to others. While she enjoys teaching, Kerrilyn is very careful not to let it encroach on her time too much, as her top priority is to make quilts. However, as time permits the making of only one heavily gridded quilt annually, Kerrilyn also enjoys excursions into quick-pieced quilts and art quilts. Her latest art quilt was part of the Breaking the Barriers mini-exhibition at Houston, Texas USA, in 1994. Totally different from her precise gridded masterpieces, this quilt involved free cutting and slashing of fabrics, and the use of wild colours.

'I loved it. It was very freeing and I was very pleased with the result,' says Kerrilyn. She feels she will continue to make these quick quilts as a foil to the more intensive work required for her gridded masterpieces.

Quilting has brought about quite dramatic changes in Kerrilyn's life:

Since I have been quiltmaking, I can get my housework done really quickly, cook really fast meals, do the washing and ironing in a flash and have no regrets when I can't go fishing with my husband and three boys. Quilting will be in my life forever. It is now part of my life and part of my family's life. My three boys now have two quilts each, with the special quilts carefully stored away from damaging light. Of course, they will all be given to the family eventually. With my studio right next to the family room, I am never isolated from the family and they are always very involved with the progress of my latest quilt.

CHAIN REACTION (above), 253 cm square, 1989
Detail from Chain Reaction (right)

BLUE AND WHITE FEATHERED STAR

225 cm square, 1992

Handmade by machine

LEE CLELAND

ANDREW PAYNE

The scene at the 1990 Quilt Show in Sydney was electric with excitement as Lee Cleland's quilt 'Blue Feathered Star' was announced as the winner of Best of Show. For the first time, a fully machine-made quilt was selected for this prestigious award. Careful examination by the many visitors to the show revealed Lee's precision in piecing and faultless machine-quilting, confirming her quilt a popular choice for the award.

Lee has always made quilts using her sewing machine. Following the instructions in a *McCalls Needlework and Crafts* magazine in 1968, she made a cot quilt for her first child, but the results left a lot to be desired. The back was puckered and nothing lay flat, but that quilt sparked the interest in quiltmaking that has become a driving force in Lee's life.

Her home became the showcase for her patchwork endeavours with beds covered by quilts made from squares, and lined and quilted curtains for the kitchen. Everything was made on the machine, quilting was 'in-the-ditch' and, according to Lee, not very accurate. But the excitement of the creative process continued.

Quite surprisingly, the local newsagent began to carry American quilting magazines, and Lee found the geometrics fascinating:

I'm not sure that I even read the instructions. I just worked out what to do myself. I drew up the cardboard templates, marked the fabric with a biro, then cut out the fabric with extra for the seam allowance. Eventually, I added a quarter inch for the seam allowance to the template and used the foot of the machine as a guide for sewing the pieces together. The techniques were very laborious and I would only tackle simple designs. With a large needle, I would tack the three layers together, taking the longest stitches possible to finish the task as quickly as possible, with a few nappy pins to hold the edges together.

Working from home, Lee continued to hone her skills on the machine, by working for an interior decorator, turning furnishing fabrics into quilted bedspreads and leftover pieces into squares for quilts.

It was quite a milestone for Lee to discover that there was a community of quilters in Australia. She was unaware that The Quilters' Guild had been established

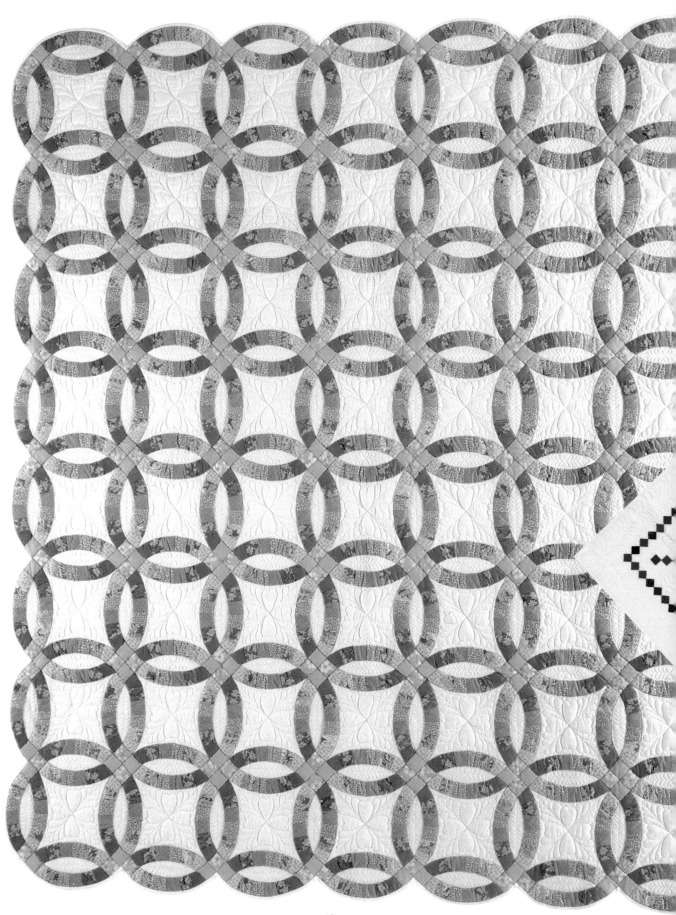

ANDREW PAYNE

in New South Wales in 1982, until their third annual members' exhibition in 1984. She describes that first exhibition as mind boggling and just couldn't believe what people were making: 'Because I had only seen quilts in books or ones I had made, I was so surprised that people were doing such diverse work. And the colours really stumped me.'

Lee came away from the exhibition with the idea that 'it's not a quilt, unless it's hand-quilted':

Nobody really said that. I just picked up the vibes that quilts had to be hand-quilted. I felt intimidated and stopped quilting for six months. I just pieced tops. I used all sorts of cotton fabrics, and the only quilt I have ever hand-quilted was made of caesarine. No wonder I didn't like the process. It was almost impossible to quilt. Other quilt tops I made used seersucker and other non-traditional fabrics. When I could get a bag of cotton scraps for a dollar, I simply couldn't see any sense in spending six dollars a metre for American cottons.

ANDREW PAYNE

Lee joined a class in English-piecing to learn how to piece by hand. She did actually finish a pincushion, but decided she felt much more at home with her machine-piecing and machine-quilting. Encouraged to follow her own inclinations, she quickly turned her accumulated tops into quilts, quilting 'in-the-ditch'.

At this stage, Lee was using cotton thread for quilting and a medium-weight polyester wadding. She quickly realised the advantage of using large safety pins to anchor the three layers prior to quilting, so she was soon able to dispense altogether with the tedious process of basting.

While she was very happy with the traditional geometric designs of her quilts, Lee felt unsure of her use of colour. She would try everything with a favourite fabric, and discard anything that was wrong, hoping that what was left was right. A course on colour with Judy Hooworth, a well-known Australian contemporary quilt artist, confirmed what she was beginning to realise: 'I am happiest working with plain fabrics, and especially like making quilts using just two colours. Blue and white is one of my favourite combinations.'

Lee moved to a new area in 1985, and with her young children now at school, she found herself with a lot of spare time. She became a regular visitor at the local patchwork shop where her skills were quickly recognised and she was soon invited to teach a class in machine-quilting:

I was petrified. I didn't even know whether machine-quilting was a skill you could learn or whether you just sat down and did it. After much preparation, and very timidly, I conducted my first class. I found it a tremendous learning experience and was very pleased I had agreed to do it.

DOUBLE WEDDING RING (far left), 185 cm x 210 cm, 1995
STAR AND CHAIN (left), 165 cm square, 1993

43

So began Lee's extensive teaching career which has taken her to most states in Australia, teaching machine-quilting and a wide range of machine-piecing classes. She was one of the tutors invited to teach at the first Australasian Symposium at Armidale in 1988, working alongside overseas tutors to provide the biggest programme of workshops ever seen in Australia: 'I was so proud to be included, I made a special vest, featuring a sewing machine appliquéd on the back, which I wore on the days I was teaching.'

Lee still teaches the basic skills used in machine-quilting in much the same way as in her first class in 1986. In a one-day workshop, Lee hits them with everything. She teaches all the techniques,

including quilting with the presser foot, and free machine-quilting: 'Then it's just practice. It's great to have a second day – then the students have a chance to practise while I'm there and if they hit a problem, I can help them.'

Initially, Lee didn't include as much free-machine-work as she was not happy with her own results, finding results of the double-line work with feathers too harsh. When a friend introduced her to monofilament thread, she realised the potential. At last, she was able to get the softness she wanted.

Over the last five years, Lee has been particularly interested in traditional quilts and with the recording of America's quilt heritage, she has had a wealth of research material available:

The more I look at and learn from these old quilts, the more I realise that the quiltmakers were very adventurous. The quilting designs are outstanding. You could not improve them in any way and the work involved is incredible.

Lee wants to continue to make quilts with a traditional feel, combining elements from these wonderful old quilts with something of herself. Sometimes she will alter the scale or change the colour and, of course, she achieves her results

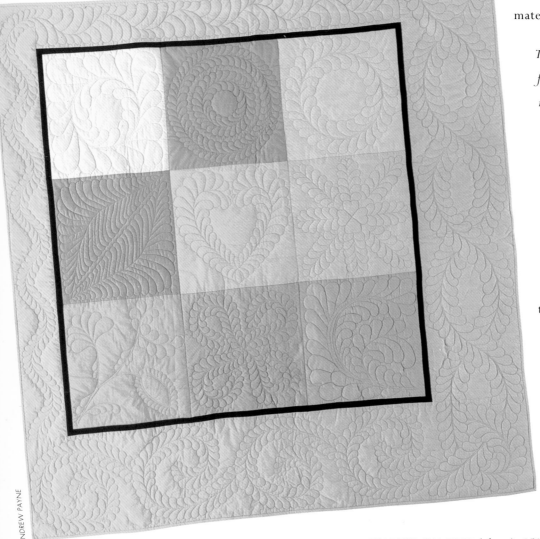

ANDREW PAYNE

FEATHER SAMPLER (*above*), *152 cm square, 1993*

with the machine. She has reverted to using a cotton thread for quilting and low-loft wadding in keeping with the traditional quilts she is replicating. During her research, Lee discovered some machine-quilted quilts from the 1880s. She found the workmanship outstanding, and the amount of quilting, done on what must have been a treadle machine, amazing: 'They are very inspirational. I will certainly be able to finish the work more quickly, but I don't feel that I could improve on the finished quilt.'

From 1991 to 1993, Lee spent most of her quilting time preparing sixty quilts for her book *Quilting Makes the Quilt*. She made each quilt design five times and quilted each of the five in a different way to demonstrate the differences quilting makes to a design. The quilt designs were traditional, but many of the quilting designs were original, designed by Lee to enhance the quilts in different ways. Lee is keen to continue developing her design skills. In fact, one of the quilting patterns in her book was taken from the stonework of a building in Washington. Lee is so pleased with her design that she is going to use it as an appliqué pattern in future work. She plans to hand-appliqué and machine-quilt, creating a new direction for her work, while still preserving the look of the traditional quilt.

Evidence of Lee's creativity is everywhere in her home. Drafted feather patterns hang on chairs and rest on the glass-topped table that often doubles as a light box when she is marking her quilts. Her studio has one table laden with sixty more quilt tops – perhaps ready for the sequel to her book. Included in this pile are five sampler quilts, the first Lee has ever made. Several 'leaving home' bags, very large patchwork bags that will hold almost anything, bulge on the shelves, full of quilts of all sizes, mostly huge:

Lee at work quilting with monofilament thread (top)
Preparing patterns for Feather Sampler (above)

I see myself as a quiltmaker rather than an artist. I am much more comfortable with homely things, but nevertheless want to make articles of excellence. Not everything I make is excellent, but I try. More than anything, I want to show people what wonderful quilting you can do with the sewing machine.

BALTIMORE

271 cm square, 1991

Magic masterpieces

KIM McLEAN

ANDREW PAYNE

Whether sitting at her computer or surrounded by a swirl of colour, Kim McLean is deep in concentration. Taking each fabric in turn, she selects or rejects it as she sees how it works on the wonderfully murky dark plaid rectangle in front of her. The contrast of the colours with the background is electric, and the combinations Kim chooses are barely believable, but they work wonderfully together.

Sprawled out on the floor, Casey, Kim's daughter, arranges and rearranges the finished squares and rectangles, offering advice on their placement. The blocks are spectacularly different. Not only has Kim made the unusual choice of muddy checks for her background with bold, almost iridescent colours for the appliqué, but then she proceeds to create the most complex blocks, setting herself a challenge other less focused quilters wouldn't consider.

Kim McLean approaches every aspect of her quiltmaking with passion. She is governed by an indefinable something. It is as though she runs and gathers everything to her as she goes. She is absolutely committed to being the very best she can be, not because of ego, but simply because she must.

As a child, Kim had all the materials available at home to investigate needlework:

I remember my mother kept a cupboard full of all sorts of sewing things — lots of material and thread — and I could just help myself whenever I wanted to. I was never allowed to have a doll, so I guess this was the substitute. It's funny though, because I can't ever remember my mother actually sewing.

During her university days, tapestry held her interest and still occupied much of her leisure time after she graduated in Pharmacy. Kim approached her profession and her craft work with the same passion for excellence, and her boundless energy made sure she achieved success in both.

Photography became a major influence in Kim's life, following a trip to Hong Kong with her husband, Ross. Seeking a pastime, Kim purchased a camera and made the decision to learn how to use it properly when she returned to Melbourne. She enrolled in a three-year diploma course which provided her with new skills which she has been able to successfully transfer to her quiltmaking:

ANDREW ELTON

CASEY, SANTA, THE BEACH – IT MUST BE CHRISTMAS,
225 cm square, 1992

In photography you have to be able to put a meaningful picture inside the frame of the camera lens and focus on exactly what it is you want to fill the space with. No cropping was allowed in our course, so it was important to get the balance of the image right. This thinking has really helped me with my quiltmaking. I can see the

image of the quilt in my head and know what the colours should be, then I have to work out how to do it.

Another important element of the photography course was black-and-white photography and the use of the grey scale, a range of grey colour from white to black: 'We were encouraged to see images devoid of colour, only registering whether an object would be light, medium or dark grey on the black-and-white film.' Kim's black-and-white photographs were prize winners and her skill in choosing fabric for her quilts according to their value – whether they are light, medium or dark – was assured.

Kim's first excursion into quiltmaking was through the purchase of a pattern to make a miniature Amish quilt, but she found the instructions very cumbersome. Next, she enrolled in a basic patchwork class and, once the tutor showed her how to draw up the blocks on graph paper, she was 'off and running': 'We were supposed to complete one block per week. I would do three or four'. At the end of the ten week course, Kim had completed two sampler quilts and entered one of these in the Beginner Quiltmaker category in The Quilt Show in Sydney in 1990, taking out first prize. With a zeal and capacity for work which would be hard to match, Kim next completed a 'Country Bride' quilt for Casey in a matter of weeks:

> I love appliqué. It's so pretty and doesn't have to be as accurate as piecing. All the pieces were basted to cardboard, following the technique I had been taught, and I would spend ages basting the pieces ready for appliqué. I made sure I had dresses with large pockets and carried my pieces with me wherever I was, so I could watch Casey and keep basting.

Few quiltmakers would choose a Baltimore quilt for their next project, having only completed two quilts, but Kim's desire to gain knowledge and experience as quickly as possible spurred her on to take up this challenge. In typical style, Kim read all she could about Baltimore quilts, before joining a class: 'I collected as many pictures of Baltimore quilts as I could and recognised the similar ideas running through them in terms of colour and design. When my research was complete, I knew what I wanted to do with my quilt.' Kim took her ideas for block and border designs with her to her very first class!

She adjusted her appliqué techniques to embrace the new method using freezer paper:

Kim chooses fabrics from her palette for her next block

ANDREW PAYNE

> Now I trace the shape onto freezer paper and cut it out. Then I iron this template onto the right side of the fabric, draw around the shape with a HB pencil and roughly cut it out leaving a seam allowance. I prepare all the shapes needed for one block. The design is marked onto the background fabric with pencil or white carbon paper, if necessary. When the shape is basted into the exact position on the background, I remove the freezer paper and trim the seam allowance, turning it under and working on only one centimetre at a time to avoid any fraying or other damage. The appliqué is then slipstitched into place. I find the whole process is very simple.

Kim finished her Baltimore quilt in seven months, just in time to send it to Lancaster in the United States in February 1991 for their quilt show. That year The Quilters Heritage Exhibition featured Baltimore quilts and Kim was keen to see how her work stood up against that of her American counterparts: 'My quilt did not receive any awards. The binding wasn't very good, but I didn't know how to do it any better at that stage. So when my quilt came back, I pulled out the binding and redid it.'

While her Baltimore quilt was still in progress, Kim tried her hand at machine-piecing. The sewing machine was not a comfortable tool for Kim, as she had always preferred to work by hand, but it did give her the opportunity to get the eighty-seven baskets needed for 'A Tisket, A Tasket, Fill Up Casey's Basket' finished in record time ready for the next step.

With the baskets completed, Kim looked for ways to fill them:

> *The first six designs were the hardest, but then I began to see pictures everywhere. Some of the designs were inspired by what I saw in quilting books, but others came from newspapers, magazines and even Casey's colouring books. I spent a lot of time reducing and enlarging designs so that they would fit into the baskets.*

Stylised flowers join a host of unusual animals to create the collection of appliqué designs adapted by Kim to fit into 'Casey's Baskets'. When all the tops were completed, Kim gave Casey the job of matching each of them to a basket. The quilt was awarded Best of Show in the 1991 Quilt Show in Sydney. At the same show, Kim's Baltimore quilt received first prize in the Appliqué section. At this stage, Kim had been making quilts for less than two years: 'Winning Best of Show was a big surprise to me, because I can see all the faults in my work, but I must say it left me feeling like I don't

have to prove anything anymore, not even to myself.'

The year 1992 saw Kim produce two more spectacular quilts. Again favouring appliqué, Kim selected one of Pat Cox's most complex designs 'The Orchid Wreath'. This breathtaking design was

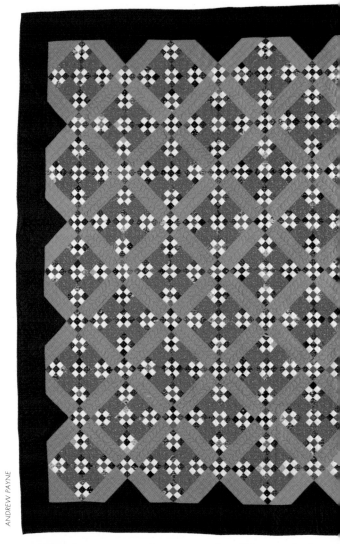

ANDREW PAYNE

extremely time-consuming, even for Kim, and she doggedly completed one cluster of orchids each week until the top was finished. The design had never been attempted before, as far as Pat is aware, because of its level of difficulty. To further enhance the quilt, Kim used extensive quilting and trapunto to make a feature of the butterflies in the quilting design. Her skills in trapunto had been finely tuned while making 'Baltimore'. Using a trial-and-error process with a new trapunto tool, Kim initially made a small hole on the back of the Baltimore: 'I was horrified – I didn't want a hole on the back of my quilt. I quickly learned to separate the weave of the fabric and insert the tool between the threads without breaking them. By the time I came to stuffing the butterflies on "The Orchid

series of books had arrived on Kim's desk before they were readily available in Australia and became the inspiration for 'Casey, Santa, The Beach, It Must Be Christmas'. The quilt was planned on paper and the large appliqué pieces made it a joy to work with for

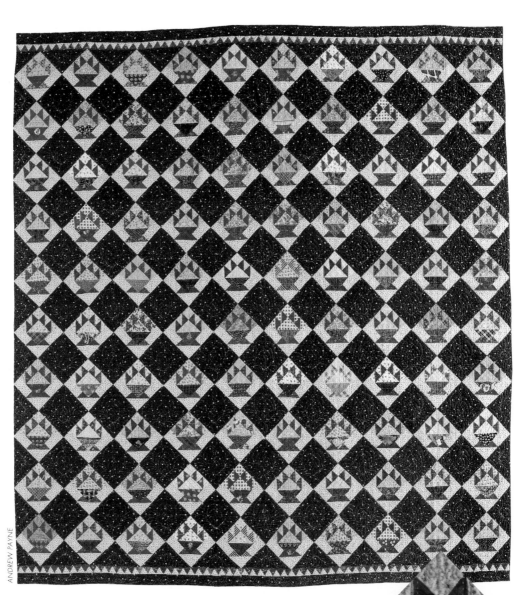

ANDREW PAYNE

BLUE AND MUSTARD SCRAP *(above left)*, *215 cm square, 1994*
SCRAP BASKET QUILT *(above)*, *225 cm x 230 cm, 1994*

Wreath", I was an expert.'

While persevering with the intricate appliqué and trapunto work required to complete 'The Orchid Wreath', Kim was working on a fun quilt, again combining appliqué and piecing. '*The Red Wagon*'

Kim after the intricacies of 'The Orchid Wreath'. The snow scenes with Santa were 'Australianised', with Santa arriving in a sled drawn by kangaroos: 'Casey chose the elements in the quilt and we had a lot

ANDREW PAYNE

of fun making it. And, of course, she chose the name.' This quilt and A Tisket, A Tasket, Fill Up Casey's Basket appeared on the cover of the *Quilter's Newsletter*.

Having made friends with her sewing machine, Kim machine-pieced the sashes to join the different-sized blocks using freezer paper. Each shape was drawn up and cut out of the freezer paper and ironed onto the fabric. The edge of the paper then became the seam guide. Kim entered both quilts in the 1992 Quilt

Show in Sydney and 'Casey, Santa, The Beach, It Must Be Christmas' won Best of Show with 'The Orchid Wreath' being awarded second place in the appliqué section.

Keen to know how she would fare in international competitions, Kim sends quilts to America each year. 'A Tisket, A Tasket, Fill Up Casey's Basket' received an honourable mention at Paducah, Kentucky in 1992 and 'The Orchid Wreath' was voted the Viewers' Choice at The Quilters Heritage Exhibition in 1993.

Kim quickly developed an international network of friends, both quilters and shop owners, enabling her to acquire books and fabrics not necessarily available in Australia. By constantly referring to these books, Kim has been able to research her latest passion for scrap quilts:

I wanted to know how to make them and everyone said to just get scraps and do it. My brain didn't click and I felt there was more to it than that. I collated information about each scrap quilt I looked at and discovered that each quilt had the same type of fabric in it. The blocks were simple and arranged in a simple design. The light, medium and dark fabrics were approximately the same colour and there was a single fabric dominating each of the blocks.

Having satisfied herself that she had the elements for a successful scrap quilt, Kim set about drafting up twelve of her favourite patterns and cutting out the templates: 'I have always loved scrap quilts and now I have the bug. When I have finished, I will have a great body of scrap quilts.'

Kim has trialled her ideas by making several scrap tops and they join her ever-increasing supply of quilts waiting to be quilted. She is planning some very special scrap quilts to add to her collection. Her latest design features a circular pattern that creates a secondary design when assembled. To prepare the templates for piecing, Kim plans to draw the design on her computer and then feed freezer paper through the printer to produce all her templates.

In spite of all she has achieved, Kim sees herself still having a long way to travel with her quiltmaking:

Having learned the basics, I now feel I want to head off in a different direction — to make quilts that say this is me. I see myself only at the beginning of my quiltmaking. It doesn't take much for me to do what I have done so far. Now I'm ready for the challenge to explore new ground and discover new ways of expressing myself. Most of my work so far has been duplicating what I have seen. I have taken elements of other people's work and combined them to make my quilts. Now I want to create my own elements. But, for me, it has been essential to understand the traditions of quiltmaking before beginning this journey.

A TISKET, A TASKET, FILL UP CASEY'S BASKET (*left*), 212 cm square, 1991
THE ORCHID WREATH (*above*), 220 cm x 250 cm, 1992

ANDREW ELTON

FRAGMENTS OF THE PAST

190 cm x 240 cm, 1994

Rags to riches

LYN INALL

ANDREW PAYNE

Recycling is an important part of the tradition of patchwork and quilting. Scraps of fabrics gleaned from old clothes or left over from dressmaking, and even old knitted garments and suiting samples have traditionally been re-used to make bedcovers. True to that tradition, Lyn Inall has taken denim jeans, perhaps the most popular item of clothing today, for her creative medium. And since denim jeans are constantly being discarded, she has a wealth of material to choose from. Lyn selects parts of the garments, such as the seams, studs, and pockets, and, utilising the texture created automatically by fraying and fading, marries them to produce her unique work.

Recycling has always been part of Lyn's life. When she was growing up in northern Queensland, Lyn made dolls' clothes and patchwork items out of discarded scraps from her mother's dressmaking. Her mother had taught her to sew straight on a treadle machine, using old needles and pages out of the magazines. Once she had perfected the required techniques, nothing could stop Lyn sewing.

Lyn's childhood interest in patchwork was revived after viewing a visiting quilt exhibition in 1985. At about this time, Lyn and her husband were planning to move to America for three years and the movie 'The Witness' with all its wonderful quilts had just been released. 'I had read some articles about the Amish and their quilts,' recalls Lyn. 'So my appetite had certainly been whetted and I decided that I would focus on learning all I could about quilting while in the United States.'

Lyn arrived in New York and had her first patchwork lesson in her first week there. From then on, she attended lots of classes. Soon, her hotel room was equipped with extra tables, an ironing board and an old sewing machine she bought for fifty dollars.

She also managed to see many quilts held by regional museums: 'The New York State Gallery has a wonderful collection, which had not been on display for two years. The staff really enjoyed showing the quilts to such an appreciative audience.'

A visit to the Balloon Fiesta in Albuquerque first introduced Lyn to the possibility of using denim in quiltmaking. The New Mexico Quilters had a stand at the Fiesta and covering their table was an unfinished patchwork denim quilt top, featuring the Double Axe

L Y N   I N A L L

design. Lyn's son, Stephen, wanted a quilt just like it. The resulting quilt, 'Always Friends', was a great success and was exhibited in the Quilt Show in Sydney in 1989. Since then, denim has been a favourite medium in Lyn's quiltmaking She has made twelve denim quilts, two of which were purchased by a group of visiting American collectors in 1994:

I enjoy the processes involved in quiltmaking. I like the challenge of drafting, drawing and calculating when I'm designing a quilt. When I'm working with denim, I mostly use traditional one-patch shapes, the Double Axe, rectangle, Batwing, trapezium, triangle or hexagon. I mark on the right side of the fabric with a blue biro, or with chalk if the fabric is very dark. It's always the cutting line I mark, so that it doesn't matter that I use biro. It is important to include the little gold additions and the orange thread, as well as the seams and pockets, to add interest to the denim. After I have cut the light, medium and dark shapes, I lay out the whole quilt. For this step, I often work outside in the garden.

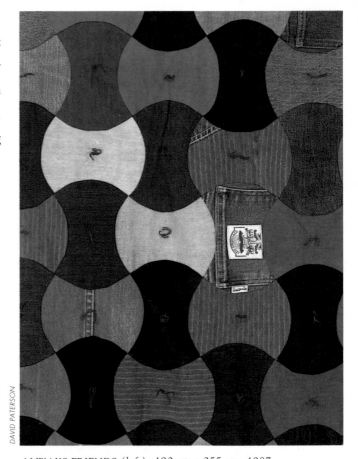

DAVID PATERSON

ALWAYS FRIENDS (*left*), 190 cm x 255 cm, 1987
Detail from Always Friends (above)

DAVID PATERSON

On her return from America in 1988, Lyn decided to share her considerable skills and, in 1989, began to teach traditional patchwork. Her classes have become her 'bread and butter'. Lyn now gives lessons at home and at an evening college four times a week.

By now, her enthusiasm for all aspects of quiltmaking knew no bounds. While in America, she had seen a jacket which employed an interesting design technique involving the use of a hexagon and strip-piecing. Adapting it to suit her needs, Lyn entered the Bernina block competition in 1989 with a block called 'Black Opal' and was successful in the Contemporary section. This was Lyn's first patchwork competition. The techniques she developed for this block – extending the sides of a shape, using different angles in the strip-piecing and including a black strip to

DAVID PATERSON

DAVID PATERSON

*Detail of Levi's Logs; the full quilt is 165 cm x 180 cm and was
completed in 1992*

*Detail from Denim Cubes
Patchwork denim bear (below)*

highlight the skewed shapes – have been used again
since then in larger pieces and Lyn still has a large
collection of 'opal' fabrics which she uses occasionally
to investigate this technique further.

In 1991, Lyn entered the National Dame Mary
Durack Outback Craft Award, and her recycled denim
quilt, 'The Mirage – An Aussie Bush Quilt' was
awarded joint third prize in the Fibre section.

Having made the decision to continue as a full-time
craftsperson on her return from overseas, Lyn has taken
every opportunity to have her work exhibited: 'I think it
is really important to show what you are doing and be
part of the overall picture. Many of my students first see
my work at shows, then want to join one of my classes.'

Lyn's quilts, along with the work of twenty-two
textile artists from various disciplines, formed a major
exhibition, Discerning Textiles – Investigations of

Process and Structure, at
the Goulburn Regional
Art Gallery in 1993. The
gallery is known for its
promotion of textiles
and this exhibition
set out to raise the
profile of con-
temporary textile
practice and to
change the perceived attitudes to textiles:

*The opportunity to participate in this exhibition was a
very important event in my textile career. As a
professional quiltmaker without any formal qualif-
ications, it was an incredible experience with all the
artists and curators working together.*

ANDREW PAYNE

THE ESSENCE OF PLACE *(far right), 124 cm x 174 cm, 1995*
Hessian bags (above), washed and ready for the construction of
Clean Straw for Nothing

Lyn prepared two pieces for the exhibition: 'Denim Cubes', a quilt using the traditional Baby Blocks pattern in two sizes, and a wallhanging, 'Denim Restructured', made from scraps of recycled denim.

For 'Denim Cubes', Lyn padded some of the pieces so that they appeared to float in the finished quilt. Lyn carefully considers all the steps in the construction when she is planning a quilt, and she is careful to avoid the need to appliqué at the end. Quilting is done by machine, or in sections with Sashiko-style quilting. Some quilts are simply tied.

Not everyone likes denim and, in classes, Lyn has often been asked for an alternative. Wool was the obvious choice as Lyn has a collection of old and new woollen fabrics. She chose the Batwing design for 'Fragments of the Past', her first bed-sized recycled wool quilt. It was awarded first place in the Other Techniques section of The Quilt Show in Sydney in

1994: 'I had previously used my collection of recycled or saved woollen fabrics to make car rugs and small lap rugs. The American collectors were keen to buy the quilt, but I couldn't sell it — it had too much of my history in it.'

Lyn constructed the quilt in much the same way as the denim Batwing, sewing dark and light shapes together. The quilt was laid out for three weeks while Lyn considered the effect. She even took photographs to see if she liked it. Finished with polyester wadding and a backing of old winter skirts, 'Fragments of the Past' is embroidered, front and back, with the first embroidery stitch Lyn learned — the twisted running stitch.

By special request, 'Fragments of the Past' went to Japan in 1995 and was part of the exhibition Yoko Sugisaki and Fifty Quilt Artists in the Saitama State Gallery of Modern Art. The exhibition included works from quiltmakers all over the world, including the work of five Australian quiltmakers, one of whom was Lyn.

Two exhibitions in 1995 were important milestones for Lyn. Women in a Changing City was held in

IRENE LORBERGS

Canberra to celebrate the twentieth anniversary of International Women's Year and featured women artists from a variety of disciplines. Lyn submitted two pieces that reached into new areas of recycling. 'Clean Straw for Nothing', representing the palliasses of our forefathers, was made from hand-stitched printed hessian bags for the top and the backing, with hand-stitched channels filled with clean straw. The other piece, 'The Essence of Place', was a quilt made from rectangles and squares of suiting fabrics, with a backing of old rayon suit lining and wool batting. Some of the suiting, sourced from discarded clothing, still retains details of pockets, cuffs, flies and creases. Lyn was lucky enough to find several rolls of suiting fabric and lining, dated 1939 and 1946, in an old tailor's shop on one of her searches for materials suitable for recycling.

The other important exhibition was Beds and Beyond – Quilts to Live With, part of the Sydney Quilt Festival held in Sydney in June, 1995. Together with three other quiltmakers, Lyn was invited to make four bed quilts, along with other smaller items, all of which were available for sale at the exhibition:

History indicates that our mothers were very capable of utilising whatever was available in order to provide the necessary creature comforts for the family. Bush quilts and waggas were constructed from fabric samples, the good parts of discarded clothing and furnishings, as well as hessian and calico bags. My work carries this tradition into the 1990s.

59

ANDREW PAYNE

BASKET MEDALLION

270 cm x 290 cm, 1994

Old quilts from new

BRIGITTE GIBLIN

ANDREW PAYNE

What do you do when you just love old quilts? Not the masterpieces destined for the museum to be admired and acclaimed for generations to come, but those wonderful old quilts that 'feather the nest', that are made to be curled up in and enjoyed. When Brigitte Giblin faced the reality that she would never be able to buy as many old quilts as she would like to own, she set about re-creating them, capturing the look and feel of the antique quilts she so admired in her work:

The more old quilts I saw, the more I wished my grandmother had owned one that I could inherit. I read lots of books recording the antique quilts of America, and they made me realise that this was what patchwork was all about. Those wonderful quilts from humble beginnings were really the quilts of history, so I began to make my own.

Brigitte has always had a love of fabric. Since childhood, the colours and textures of fabric have held a certain magic for her. When she was eighteen, she stayed with her aunt in France for six years, absorbing the local culture and spending time each day at the aunt's dressmaking studio:

I loved all the fabric and the buttons and watching the women making all those incredible garments for the salon. My aunt, who worked a very long full day, was always excited about any new fabrics that came in. She would call me over, inviting me to feel the fabric. It is her I thank for my love of fabric. Even now, I occasionally get a pack of the most wonderful pieces from her.

France has a rich heritage of interesting fabrics and Brigitte has been inspired by her visits to the old homes in the south of France, where she even found some patchwork quilts made from stunning old fabrics.

Her own quiltmaking career began quite traditionally. She was among the first students of Di Chalinor, one of the original teachers of patchwork in Australia. 'It was in the very early days of patchwork, with lots of green and apricot quilts and Liberty fabrics,' recalls Brigitte. 'I did the usual things, progressing to quick machine-piecing, making tops in a weekend, and using lots of checks and plaids to create very country-looking quilts'.

Fabric continued to fascinate Brigitte, and any new fabric range had to be immediately turned into a quilt

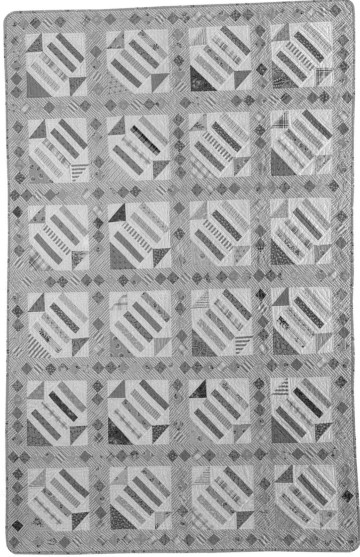

ANDREW PAYNE

1930S SCRAP BAG, 135 cm x 195 cm, 1993

sister-in-law, Julie Roberts. Opened in 1991, this shop provided the best in children's clothes, as well as quilts and quiltmaking supplies. Not only was this a unique concept, but the quilts side of the business was beginning to reveal Brigitte's touch of magic when it came to selecting fabrics. Only having half a shop to fill with bolts of fabric, Brigitte had to be very selective. Somehow what she chose was always just what her customers were looking for. Eventually when the business became The Country Sampler, entirely devoted to quiltmaking, Brigitte had developed a reputation for making quilts look old. Visitors to her shop would ask if the quilts decorating the shop were antique or not. One quilt, 'Pine Trees', was so popular, that Brigitte turned it into a kit, selling dozens of them to her customers.

She was also developing a reputation for her designs for country-look home accessories, including a sewing machine cover, stencilled cushions and rag baskets. These were also very popular kits and Brigitte spent many hours cutting and packaging, so that others could enjoy her wonderful fabric selections.

top. Brigitte remembers, 'I couldn't get enough quilts, so I would satisfy the urge to try all the new fabrics by machine-piecing lots of tops'.

Already her ability to choose fabrics that worked together was evident. At the same time she was hand-piecing and creating wonderful country quilts, like the cerise 'Square in a Square', which she completed travelling to and from work.

With the birth of her third child, Brigitte decided to leave her high-powered position as an events coordinator and open her own patchwork shop. Kids and Quilts was an exciting venture for Brigitte and her

More and more Brigitte was drawn to old quilts, really wanting to capture the look of those wonderful old quilts:

Some of my friends have antique quilts, and they introduced me to different tastes in quilts. Even at exhibitions, I can admire the workmanship of the modern quilts, but I am rarely taken by a quilt enough to want to take it home with me. But I really wanted to take all the old quilts home.

After two years of the frantic pace of a quilt shop, the preparation of class samples and the filling of orders for her country kits, Brigitte decided to slow down. 'In my frantic state to try all the fabrics and make all the quilts, I'd forgotten to enjoy the process', she admits.

In her pocket, Brigitte had been carrying around a postcard of a wonderful old quilt, made by Florence Peto, which she decided to make by hand. The centre of the quilt had twelve naive blocks, and Brigitte often took out the picture to examine yet again the mix of fabrics, and the design features that had captivated her. Long before the quilt was started, she had begun collecting fabrics she felt would work in the quilt: 'I looked for lots of old-fashioned calicos, with small floral prints, and mixed them with a few checks and a few stripes that look like shirting. I chose fabrics that looked like they had been around for hundreds of years.' The postcard didn't include a pattern or instructions, but Brigitte, who loves drafting her own patterns, was unfazed.

The border of dollies holding hands was determined so they would fit beautifully around the border, so Brigitte had to work backwards, fitting the blocks into the space left in the centre. Having carefully chosen fabrics to achieve that wonderful naive look, Brigitte added the extra dimension by using a cotton batt. When the quilt was finished, all Brigitte's children tried to claim it, but Brigitte was emphatic: 'I made 'Dollies' just for me. I wanted to quilt for my own pleasure, not to make another quilt for one of the children. I made it for me, just because I love it.'

TOILE STRIPPY,
160 cm x 195 cm, 1993

Brigitte quilts without a hoop and follows no drawn lines, preferring to allow the piecing or appliqué to dictate where the quilting will be. When eyebrows are raised at this unorthodox approach, Brigitte explains that she is all for the simplest methods possible: 'As long as it's quilted, that's the main thing.'

She uses the longest needle possible to quilt with, preferring a number nine crewel needle to the number twelve betweens usually chosen by quilters. Brigitte claims that the tiny needles get lost in her big hands! With her long needle she is able to take six to eight stitches at a time.

ANDREW PAYNE

Her lines of quilting are very close together, an essential when using cotton wadding.

One of the endearing features of antique quilts is the crinkling of the surface due to the constant laundering and wear. Brigitte has developed a method of producing this effect in a new quilt:

I had quilted '1930s Scrap Bag' before 'Dollies', using a cotton batt to give me that antique look and feel. When the quilt was completed, I wet it, then immediately put it in a hot tumble drier. Then I watched and waited, checking every fifteen minutes to see if I had ruined the quilt. It came out all crinkled and beautiful. I was so excited. It worked and I'd been game enough to try.

Brigitte takes great care to get just the right mix of fabric: too many checks will make a modern country quilt. So when she is teaching her students about fabric, she begins by inviting them to pick three fabrics and sometimes changes their choices to get a better mix, adding quite unexpected fabrics. Her students claim that they never look at fabric in the same way after Brigitte's classes:

A lot of people start with fabrics that coordinate, but they end up with a decorator sheet, not a naive quilt. People have to learn to improvise. If you run out of fabric in naive work, you can just add something else and it looks like it is meant to be there.

Brigitte imagines her quilts as a black-and-white photograph. If the blocks appear as the same shade of grey, then the quilt is a failure. She really likes to use black, with busy prints to give texture, and some sort of spark to make it interesting. 'Originally', Brigitte insists, 'quilts were made from scraps, from what you had in your bag of bits at the time. So I like to use lots of

ANDREW PAYNE

disjointed fabrics in my naive work, with black to give the sharpness.' She enjoys using cream and black fabrics, and murky browns. Very strong colours are used in small pieces and she stays away from modern colours, like aqua:

The fabrics need to be mellow, with a certain warmth. I don't tea-dye any fabrics, so I just keep looking for the right fabric. I have discovered that there are many people like me who have done lots of machine-made quilts, and just want to quilt for pleasure. Over one hundred people have attempted 'Dancing

Brigitte sits quilting, surrounded by examples of her work (inset)
BIRDS IN MY GARDEN *125 cm square, 1995*

ANDREW PAYNE

64

PINE TREES, *140 cm square, 1992*

ANDREW PAYNE

library, particularly the books recording the historic quilts from each State in the United States and *The History of Cloth and Comfort* by Roderick Kiracose. When she is planning a new quilt, the books are put away and Brigitte comes up with her own ideas. She explains: 'I might have something I've seen on one quilt, and a little of another. It still has my stamp on it.'

Brigitte's latest project is a sampler featuring small blocks, again in a naive style. The whole quilt is planned roughly on paper, just a sketch to define the concept. For this quilt, Brigitte must choose seventy-two traditional blocks. For each one, she drafts an accurate pattern on graph paper and prepares templates from template plastic. The fabric is marked on the back in the traditional way and the block is hand-pieced. All these tiny blocks need to be made before the assembling of the quilt can begin:

Dollies', and most have captured the look of the old quilt. Their enthusiasm grows and grows and they can't wait to get the quilt together. It doesn't bother me that people are copying my work. After all, I get my ideas from old quilts in publications. This is one of the nice things about quilting, and it's flattering to think that my work has inspired other people.

Brigitte doesn't actually copy the quilts she sees. She looks at lots of pictures from the books in her extensive

I feel as though I'm inspiring a different love of quilting. I am trying to go back to grass roots. It is lovely to meet with other women, share ideas and get excited about a piece of fabric. You can really get into it, have an avenue of artistic expression and have something to show for it at the end of the day. For many women, there isn't a lot to show for all their hard work in life. A quilt is something that you can show to others and have them tell you how clever you are! Only women who quilt can understand.

DANCING DOLLIES SAMPLER, *140 cm x 170 cm, 1993*

ANDREW PAYNE

HUGS AND KISSES ALL OVER OZ

210 cm square, 1992-1995

Scrap happy

JAN URQUHART

ANDREW PAYNE

The town of Roma will never forget the Queensland Quilters' Touring Tutors. Caught in the grip of drought in 1990, north-west Queensland was parched and dry. But, when Jan Urquhart's decorated four-wheel drive rolled into town, packed with patchwork paraphernalia and quilts, the whole town turned out to greet them — so did the rain. Jan and Helen Kingcott, her travelling companion and tyre changer, couldn't have been made more welcome. Jan likes to boast that she broke the drought!

Some very funny things happened while we were on tour. We had been driving around Emerald, following a fairly suspect map, when we finally found the house we had been looking for. As we got out of the car, our hostess grabbed us, dragging us towards the house and into her kitchen which was overflowing with soap suds. Apparently, someone put ordinary dish-washing liquid in her dishwasher. We all had to bale furiously. Needless to say we all became great friends.

The effects of the drought were everywhere, but, in spite of these difficult circumstances, women came eagerly to Jan's Recession Buster class. No-one was allowed to bring any matching fabric, only scraps. Jan went through one lady's fabrics at Mount Isa and told her to put all her coordinated apricot and green fabrics away! Jan suggested the lady dig out all her scraps, and the fabrics she didn't like or didn't know what to do with, and take those to the workshop instead:

Touring the countryside teaching patchwork is a far cry from accountancy, Jan's chosen profession. For several years she was coordinator for a TAFE college in Sydney, teaching clerical procedures while maintaining her part-time job with an interior decorator. Jan loved both jobs. Together, these experiences built her confidence in her teaching ability and her colour sense, essential skills for the successful quiltmaker and tutor.

Jan has always had an interest in craft. She was first introduced to patchwork in 1982:

My mother showed me a hexagon quilt in a magazine and since it was a craft that was new to me I decided to try it out. My first quilt (which is on my bed) was pieced over papers. I had used Rolling Star as the pattern, although I didn't know that it had a name. I thought I was so clever working it out, not realising it was a traditional pattern.

Jan's next contact with quiltmaking was at a patchwork shop on the Gold Coast in Queensland. In the shop, there were some examples of crazy patchwork, and Jan bought a book explaining some of the techniques. Not understanding that the American term for calico was muslin, Jan built her crazy patchwork stole onto a foundation of butter muslin, and took it with her when she attended her first Queensland Quilters meeting:

ANDREW PAYNE

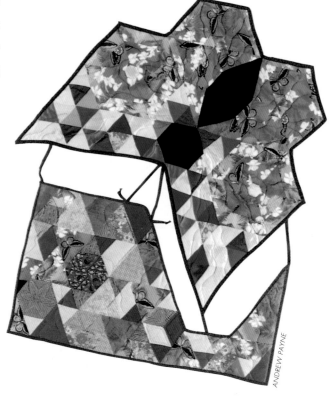

ANDREW PAYNE

They said to bring along some lunch and show and tell. I laughed. It sounded just like kindergarten. The only thing I was game to take was my crazy patchwork stole. It was a great success. Everyone was very complimentary. No one criticised anyone's work. Wherever you were at with your patchwork was fine with them. It felt like home.

At that meeting, Jan also discovered that you could use a running stitch to sew pieces together. She was so excited, she made a quilt top in two weeks and never went back to piecing with papers again. Less than a month after joining the Queensland Quilters, Jan was the group's treasurer!

The more Jan became involved in making quilts, the less satisfied she was with her job as an accountant. Finally, she

THE CHARM OF JACOB IS NOT A PUZZLE – IT'S A-MAZING (*left*), 150 cm x 180 cm, 1991
HEXAGON FLUTTERBY (*above*), 1989

decided to give up accountancy altogether and became a full-time quiltmaker – despite the misgivings of her loving family.

Jan sold her first quilt during Heritage Week in 1989. The design, using Colonial House blocks, was based on the houses in her street. Soon her days were filled with making collars, bags and quilts to stock various street stalls.

Jan also decided to become a teacher. As the resident teacher at the local patchwork shop, Jan began teaching basic skills, and quilts using Sarah Nephew's sixty-degree triangle. Always keen to fully investigate a topic, Jan looked at design work using the sixty-degree triangle, the use of different scales, rotating the triangle, and making three-dimensional designs – even before this information was available in print.

A commission to make a quilt caused Jan to rethink the way she used fabric in her quilts. The fabrics chosen by the husband and wife just would not work together, so Jan began to investigate why some fabrics will work together and others wouldn't. She discovered colour value and was able to explain the problem to her clients. Her popular workshop, 'Listen With Your Eyes' is all about colour value:

People get so bogged down with matching fabrics. I encourage them to go with their instincts. Different fabrics can do the same job and the important thing is how dark and light the fabric is, not necessarily what colour it is. I try to encourage people to have a go, even if they are unsure.

After a while they get the idea that any of the blocks will go together, if the tones are right.

The basis of all Jan's work with scrap quilts is to reduce any traditional block to squares and rectangles, and to simply cut light and dark pieces with no regard to the pattern or colour of the fabric. All the pieces are cut with a rotary cutter and machine-sewn.

Jan is an enthusiastic goal setter and believes that all quilters are goal setters: 'They put tiny pieces of fabric together into a block. They don't actually make a quilt. They do little bits at a time in very small steps. This is how I run my life. I like to identify what I really want, find a way to make it happen and then find the people who can help me.'

This is the approach Jan used when she decided to

Jan's latest work in progress featuring a traditional pattern and using non-traditional fabrics

ANDREW PAYNE

write a book, after only two years of quiltmaking. Many of her students had been so impressed with her workshops that Jan decided to put her ideas into a book, *Designing Quilts is Fun – Sets and Borders*. Having never written before, she decided that not only did she want to be a writer, but that she *was* a writer and would write one page each day. Her daughter became her illustrator and another friend did the typesetting. The book, self-published, became a reality. Jan has continued her writing career, contributing a regular column to *Down Under Quilts*, Australia's first patchwork magazine.

Her computer became another challenge, another opportunity to practise her goal-setting skills. Jan became engrossed in finding out all she could about its application to quiltmaking, and regularly illustrates her column using a variety of quilting programs. Her expertise is often called on to give reviews on new software for quilters.

While still living in Queensland, Jan was involved with Craft Criticism, a group of textile artists who meet to review and offer criticism of each other's work: 'It really helped to gel my ideas, to help me focus. I feel everything you do influences the way you work, that nothing is for nothing. All your experiences get stirred up and you don't know what will come out.' She would like to see a similar group formed in Sydney.

Jan has received many accolades during her twelve years of quiltmaking, not least of these being an invitation to participate in South Bank Impressions – an exhibition of vibrant textile works, arranged by the Queensland Arts Council. Her quilt, 'Let's See What's on the South Bank', made from scrappy triangles

ANDREW PAYNE

cleverly arranged, creates impressions of people engaged in all sorts of activities. Hand-quilting adds the third dimension, creating further images.

Jan just loves to use scraps, and her quilts are full of fabrics that hold special meaning. 'The Charm of Jacob is not a Puzzle – It's a-Mazing', a special quilt she made for her grandson, has pieces of fabric representing different members of his family, including one with cotton reels for great grandma.

The mix of large print fabrics so favoured by Jan is evident in 'Ode to Joy (Song to the Unknown Quiltmaker)'. This quilt received second prize in the Dame Mary Durack Outback Craft Awards in 1991. Jan had to enter the quilt in the Knitting and Tapestry Section, since there was no patchwork and quilting category, a situation that has since been remedied.

'Hugs and Kisses All Over Oz' was pieced from collected scraps over a four-year period. Most of the pieces for this quilt were gathered during Jan's outback teaching trips. When Jan's daughter Rachel was to be married, she chose lots of fabric from the stash in Jan's workroom.

'I'll have some of that and a bit of that' she said, as she raided the supply. Much to Jan's delight, Rachel chose many of Jan's favourite florals.

Collected fabrics, stored and treasured – not for their value, but for their significance – have always been an important part of the quilting story:

It is my belief that many people come to quiltmaking believing that they will be able to use their collected fabrics, their saved up bits. My first quilt was made from old batik dresses and lots of my quilts have pieces in them that are significant, coming from different

sources. Originally people made quilts with what they had on hand. They weren't looking at it as art, even though they were involved in an art form. But that isn't what they were about. I think that we are still making quilts that way.

LISTEN WITH YOUR EYES *(above left)*, 135 cm square,1990
RACHEL'S WEDDING QUILT *(left)*, 210 cm square, 1993
Jan hand-quilting the border of one of her quilts

NEW YORK BEAUTY

65 cm square, 1993

Tiny treasures

VIRGINIA ENRIGHT

NEIL LORIMER

Virginia Enright is passionate about small things. Clusters of miniature quilting hoops hold her tiny quilts, creating lovely nooks in her home. In one corner, she has tucked a Log Cabin quilt under the needle of a child's sewing machine, and included a miniature iron and even small bundles of fabric as part of the display. Everything has a place.

Virginia's work space is her dining-room table. Virginia feels that this limited space, in part, accounts for her working in miniature, re-creating traditional quilts in a tiny form: 'Every night I need to clear the table for the family dinner. To be able to cut out a whole quilt, then store it in an ice-cream container has certain advantages.'

Virginia's first attempts at patchwork were Grandmother's Flower Garden blocks made with multi-coloured hexagons:

My great-aunt's next-door neighbour inspired me to begin. She made yo-yo tops out of wonderful coloured circles and I loved the patterns she created. I managed to finish six flowers in red, white and black before investigating other forms of patchwork.

Spurred by her first efforts and buoyed by her natural enthusiasm, Virginia turned her attentions to traditional quilt blocks:

My first pieced blocks were also red, black and white, the colours of my bedroom. I'm still quite impressed with my efforts, as I only had a picture in an American magazine to follow and my knowledge didn't extend to drafting on graph paper or working with quarter-inch seam allowances.

Sewing was considered an essential pastime in Virginia's home, as she was growing up. All the clothing was made at home and the clear lesson was ' If you need it, don't buy it, make it'. Her own sewing skills were slow to develop, with her teachers despairing of her ever producing anything acceptable. As a left-hander, Virginia had to really work hard to accomplish what others seemed to find so easy:'I wish my teachers could see me now. Boy, would they be surprised!'

When she was eighteen, Virginia moved to New York to live with her aunt: 'There were lots of quilts around and I thought they were all lovely. There was never a question of buying a quilt, but always the encouragement to make one.' With no patchwork shops in her neighbourhood, Virginia had to wait until she returned to Australia to learn the skills necessary to make her own quilts.

Back in Melbourne in 1981 after the birth of her first daughter, Virginia took her initial patchwork class. Her teacher had learned patchwork with Beth Gutcheon whose book *The Perfect Patchwork Primer* was used as a textbook. Everyone in the class was doing something different and Virginia chose to make pieced Clay's Choice blocks in red, white and blue:

It was a really good group to be part of. There was a lot of encouragement to follow your own ideas. We were taught the basics of patchwork using a repeat block of our own choice. No-one used pastel fabrics or made a sampler quilt.

Such was Virginia's enthusiasm for the lessons that she drove one hour each way to the classes in one of Melbourne's coldest winters. While the group cut out or stitched, their teacher read inspirational material from *The Quilters – Women and Domestic Art*. These poignant stories told of women living in impoverished circumstances who made quilts, often providing them with their only comfort.

From the beginning, Virginia's quilts were machine-pieced and hand-quilted. Slowly, she completed a quilt for each of her children, juggling her quilting time with family duties.

NEIL LORRIMER

TOKYO LADY (*above*), 24 cm x 27.5 cm, 1994
CYANOTYPE STAR (*right*), 24 cm square 1994
CRAZY CRAYONS (*far right*), 26 cm square, 1994

NEIL LORRIMER

In 1987, with Christmas just around the corner, Virginia decided to add a quilt to her festive decorations: 'I had been reading Becky Schaefer's book, *Working in Miniature* and really loved the look of the tiny quilts. So I decided to make a miniature Christmas tree quilt.'

Adapting the suggested methods to suit her own preferences, Virginia finished her first tiny quilt in record time; others quickly followed. However,

Virginia often found the template-free method of piecing very awkward, especially for very tiny pieces. She looked for an easier way to get an accurate result. Rather than using half-square triangles, she began to use rectangles with squares to get her tiny triangles: 'I cut the square the same width as the rectangle and place it on the end of the rectangle. I sew along the diagonal of the square and when the seam is trimmed, I have the perfect triangle.'

Left are the steps Virginia followed to produce a block for the quilt shown opposite. These are (clockwise from top left) accurate diagram on graph paper, full-size drawing on interfacing, the attached pieces, assembling the block Virginia's partly completed quilt including the House block (below left)

Ideas for improving her techniques, making her miniatures easier to construct, kept surfacing. In 1988, Virginia read an article by Debbie Hall on foundation papers for patchwork. Here the pattern is drawn accurately on paper and photocopied as many times as needed. Fabric is then sewn along the drawn lines and when the block is completed the paper is removed. Virginia used this method in her classes, teaching her students to use foundation papers for big projects, especially Log Cabin quilts, while continuing to use quick-piecing methods for miniatures:

Finally the penny dropped — I could use foundation papers for my miniatures, as well. I was making a name badge for myself to take on a trip to America. It was a very tiny miniature and I could see that it would be much easier to work on foundation papers than trying to use quick-piecing methods. The accuracy was amazing, and even a novice could do it.

Virginia's penchant for small things is not confined to her quilt-making. She also makes dolls and bears, and has noticed over the years that if she makes a doll she usually makes a tiny version

NEIL LORIMER

soon afterwards. She especially loves making three-inch jointed bears.

In 1992, Waverly Patchworkers in Melbourne distributed fabrics for their challenge, which set Virginia thinking along another new path:

I decided to astound everyone and make a Pineapple quilt only 15 cm square, with logs 3 mm wide. There was no way I could get the accuracy I wanted using foundation papers. The paper would either rip, sewing such tiny pieces, or be impossible to remove after the sewing was finished. I solved that problem by replacing the paper with interfacing. Firstly, I draw the design accurately on graph paper, then I trace it onto the interfacing. Next, I attach the pieces of fabric on the opposite side to the design I have drawn, sewing along the drawn lines This way I don't have to cut the pieces accurately, just make sure I have enough fabric to allow for seams. The quilt, with its three hundred and sixty-nine pieces, was awarded first prize in the Waverly Patchworkers Challenge — even though the yellow and blue challenge fabrics are barely visible!

Virginia has adapted her technique to enable her to complete most traditional blocks. For The House, the four rectangular sections are pieced separately, then stitched together. Working from left to right, each piece is sewn into place. As the work progresses, it looks very untidy. But when the sections are finally sewn together, Virginia achieves a very accurate result. Only then is the excess fabric trimmed: 'I introduced this technique to my students calling it, "The Sloppy Girl's Guide to Accurate Patchwork".'

Virginia is convinced the most important element when working in miniature is colour and, in particular, having a high contrast background to show off the piecing. Without this strong contrast, the definition of the piece is lost.

COUNTRY HOMESTEAD *(top), 5 cm square, 1994*
A collection of Virginia's tiny quilts (above)

Virginia is a much sought-after tutor, regularly included in weekend programmes by both state and interstate guilds as well as working for local patchwork shops. Her most popular class is, of course, Miniatures. Teaching has led her to write articles and to prepare projects for Australian and overseas publications. She also exhibited her work as one of The Textile Trio, which included Margaret Furness, wearable art designer, and Cheryl Skewes, accessories designer:

I always feel I am the one who has gained from teaching. I love the friendships I have formed with quilters all over Victoria and many other parts of Australia. When I teach, I like to give my students ideas to develop rather than just teaching a certain quilt. As my students ask to be shown new things, they push me into exploring different areas. Of course, while I am researching new ideas to present to my students, I am storing up ideas to follow for myself.

Most recently, Virginia has been involved in an art course at Deakin University. She had originally thought that she would not be interested in the parts of the course that covered drawing and watercolours, but she found that the techniques of drawing, relating to light and tone, can be readily applied to patchwork. Virginia particularly enjoyed dyeing and printmaking and plans to create her own fabrics, using her new-found skills; for her miniature work 'an A4-sized piece of fabric lasts for ages'.

Already the scope for using self-created fabrics is becoming apparent in Virginia's work. She has featured a cyanotype centre in her quilt 'Contemporary Sawtooth', and plans to feature many others of her prepared fabrics in future pieces. At the end of the

NEIL LORIMER

AROUND THE TWIST (*above*), 17.5 cm x 20 cm, 1993
MINIATURE PINEAPPLE (*right*), 16 cm square, 1992
RAINBOW FLYING GEESE (*bottom right*) 18 cm x 25 cm, 1993

course, students (including Virginia) participated in an exhibition of work:

It was a wonderful experience to be involved in. There were several embroiderers in our course, and I saw some very innovative embroidery techniques. I'm keeping those on the back-burner for future reference.

The future waits to be unfurled for Virginia. She continues to look for simple, innovative ways to complete her tiny projects. Her passion for traditional and tiny quilts has not been lessened by the inclusion of her own fabrics in her work or by combining patchwork with embroidery. Rather the possibilities for creativity have been broadened and enhanced, and Virginia's appetite whetted for future projects, beginning, as always, with a traditional pattern.

NEIL LORIMER

NEIL LORIMER

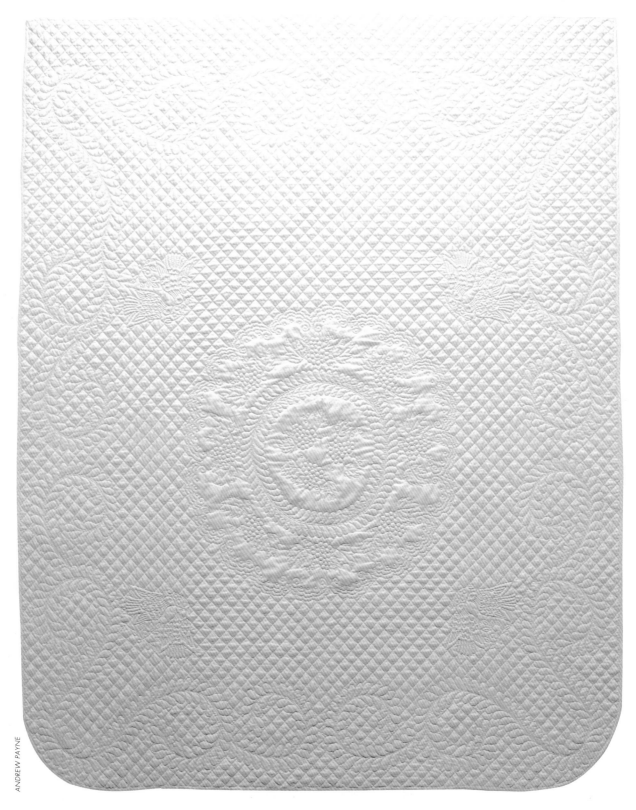

THE ANNIVERSARY QUILT

220 cm square, 1986

ANDREW PAYNE

White on white

N A R E L L E   G R I E V E

ANDREW PAYNE

Narelle Grieve is a traditional quilt-maker. She makes no apology for this and, while perfecting her own work, continually encourages others to learn the basic skills of patchwork and quilting, and to strive for excellence. Her work with white whole-cloth quilts displays a level of perfection achieved by few quilters, and continues to amaze and inspire those who give her quilts close inspection. People simply cannot believe that her tiny stitches have been achieved by hand.

Narelle learned to make quilts in the United States while living there with her husband and three daughters. It was while she was there that she won what was to be the first of her many quilting awards:

I had to drive to the evening college through sleet and snow and virtually slid into class. We were making an Amish Basket and I was the only one who finished, because I had nothing else to do. My house was completely empty, as we were still waiting for our furniture to arrive. Everyone from the other one hundred and twenty classes that were part of the night school voted on our work at the end of term, and my quilt won!

Patchwork and quilting had undergone a revival in the United States during the bicentenary celebrations in 1976, so Narelle found many classes to attend. All the quiltmaking being done at that time was by hand with very little machine-piecing and almost no machine-quilting. Narelle soon began teaching and enrolled in the Accredited Teacher Program run by the National Quilting Association. 'I was really nervous', she remembers, 'because I hadn't done an exam since Methuselah was a boy. I needed to present samples of my work, together with my teaching notes and then go for an interview to explain my teaching techniques. They liked my work and I passed.'

Narelle joined the Mainline Quilters in Philadelphia, where she enjoyed the company of fellow quilters at meetings and on excursions to quilt shows. It was at one of these shows that Narelle saw her first wholecloth quilt: 'I just couldn't believe it. I knew straight away that this was what I wanted to do.'

Narelle knew she didn't want to make her quilt out of cotton and she searched for a suitable fabric with a sheen that was easy-care. Eventually, she found a fabric which is now available in Australia as 'Narelle' fabric.

ANDREW PAYNE

ANDREW PAYNE

K. SCHWERDTFEGER

Next, a friend introduced Narelle to Mrs Sammy King, an Amish lady who marked wholecloth quilts:

We went to her very Amish home and she began to pull out a huge roll of patterns from beside her bed and started laying them out. At this stage, I didn't know what I wanted on my quilt, then I saw the feathered wreath and decided to use that as the centre with more feathered wreaths around the border and birds in the corner.

Mrs King marked Narelle's top with dressmaker's carbon and a pencil on her big kitchen table.

'The Anniversary Quilt', as Narelle named this first wholecloth quilt, won Best of Show at two quilt shows in America and was placed in the stand of Excellence at the Royal Easter Show in Sydney in 1988:

When I was quilting The Anniversary Quilt, I used a large floor frame and started in the middle and worked towards the end, so in fact I had not seen any large section of the quilt finished. When my husband, Ian, and I unrolled it so that I could work on the other end, I was really pleased and very excited with what I was seeing for the first time. Ian said he thought it was nice. You can imagine how impressed I was with this comment! After that, I called the quilt 'The Nice Anniversary Quilt'.

Sewing had always been part of Narelle's life. Her mother was a keen sewer and always kept the sewing machine out and available for use. She had even made

Narelle a crazy-patch apron for her trousseau and had dabbled in patchwork with hexagon quilts. Narelle sewed clothes for herself and her children and her home is decorated with her needlework pieces in tapestry and cross stitch. The exquisite tapestry on her dining-room chairs was lovingly worked by Narelle. Her love of old textiles is also evident in the collection of framed pieces on display, rescued from many sources, along with her collections of country memorabilia.

While she was happy to admit to her expertise in needlework, Narelle never saw herself as creative, just good at working in a grid, or following a pattern. It was not until she began to make her white-on-white quilts and to design her own patterns that she was prepared to recognise her own creativity: 'At school, I had accepted that I was not creative because I couldn't draw and, although I always sewed, I didn't think that was creative. Quilting has made me realise that sewing can be very creative.'

I LOVE OLD PLASTER CEILINGS (*top left*), *242 cm x 250 cm, 1989*
Narelle sits working the tiny quilting stitches for which she is renowned (left)
OLD HOUSES OF AUSTRALIA (*above*), *134 cm square, 1988*

Back in Australia in 1987, Narelle found a healthy community of quilters and joined the Quilters' Guild of New South Wales. She became the president of the Guild in 1989/90, and initiated many innovative programmes. Having recognised the value of the teacher accreditation programme in the United States, she began a similar programme in Australia to ensure that the basic skills of patchwork were being taught well by adequate teachers.

Always keen to encourage quilt-makers to strive for a higher standard in their quiltmaking, Narelle was instrumental in establishing judging as a feature of the annual Members' Quilt Show, which now attracts national and international entries with prize money in excess of ten thousand dollars.

Quilt valuation was also an important issue for Narelle and, in 1990, she invited all the state guilds to meet to discuss the need for a national scheme for valuation. This gathering became the first meeting of what is now known as The National Council of Quilters which meets annually to share and exchange ideas. While a national valuation scheme has not been adopted, each state now has a system for valuing quilts which is accepted by the other states.

While being passionate about traditional quiltmaking, as president of the Guild, Narelle was very aware of the need to have a broader vision that encompassed all facets of quiltmaking. As a result, when Judy Hooworth and Anna Brown, internationally known fibre artists, approached Narelle about including an exhibition of contemporary quilts as part of the Guild's calendar, Narelle agreed. So began The New Quilt exhibitions, held annually at the Manly Art Gallery in Sydney. This exhibition has achieved national

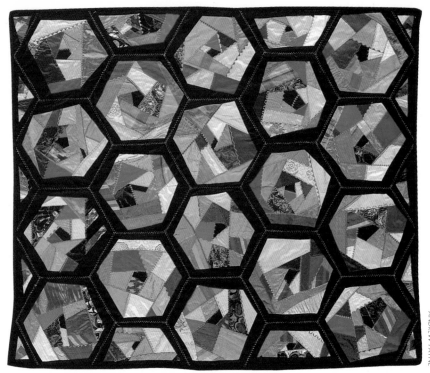

ANDREW PAYNE

A LITTLE BIT OF CRAZY (2), *85 cm x 100 cm, 1993*

recognition as the showcase for contemporary quiltmaking in Australia.

Not only does Narelle make wonderful traditional quilts, but she collects them:

That first quilt was the hardest to buy. At a YWCA boot sale in a wonderful old house in Philadelphia, I found an Irish Chain quilt that had been quilted to within an inch of its life. I ummed and aahhhed and finally bought it. Now I don't hesitate. I know what I want to spend and I look for quilts that have a different pattern from the ones I already have. I have to really like the quilts that I buy — which are mostly hand-pieced and hand-quilted. Many of the quilts are unsigned and even fewer of them say where they were made. I guess they just assumed that everyone knew that Aunt Bessie lived in Ohio, so why put it on the quilt. They weren't making heirlooms they were just making bed covers to keep their family warm.

As interest in and prices for old quilts have risen in recent years, Narelle has started to collect quilt tops.

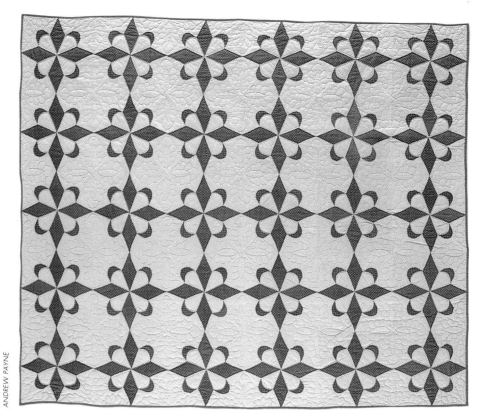

ANDREW PAYNE

An antique Star and Cresent quilt top, completed and quilted by Narelle

owner loaned me the cornices and the large central piece and I had them drawn. Then I enlarged and reduced the drawing so that it would fit where I wanted it. There is always a lot of planning and preparation for a wholecloth quilt. I get ideas from books and use tracing paper and lots of photocopying to get exactly what I want. For the pressed tin ceilings from Calrossie School, I worked from a photograph. Everything was measured and kept to scale and then enlarged and reduced as needed. I only needed to prepare one-quarter of the design and then trace it onto the fabric using a propelling pencil.

Some of these she has turned into finished quilts, saying, 'the lady who pieced the top hoped one day to finish it. I feel she can rest knowing her quilt is in the hands of someone who loves it. It's rather nice to think that I have finished her work for her.'

One of Narelle's most exciting buys was in Sydney when she discovered an old Welsh Durham quilt at a garage sale. The quilt is believed to have been made in Wales during the Rural Industries Bureau Scheme in the 1920s and 1930s. It is of considerable historic importance because it is the only known example of Miss G. K. Evans's work. Previously, there was only a photograph of her work in the Victoria and Albert museum.

Narelle continued to make her own wholecloth quilts. The second large white-on-white quilt was 'I Love Old Plaster Ceilings':

I borrowed all the plaster pieces I needed from a factory that has been there 'since pussy was a kitten'. The

Recently, Narelle has discovered that the Powerhouse Museum in Sydney has a copy of the Wunderlich catalogue with all the patterns for the pressed tin used in many of Australia's old houses. Narelle stitches these quilts with stipple-quilting, so closely worked that it resembles the markings on the pressed tin.

Narelle feels that quiltmaking has made an incredible difference in her life:

I am much more confident and enjoy meeting new people. I guess moving to America with no family support meant I had to become self-sufficient. I was able to travel far and wide to see quilt shows, museums and second-hand shops, and Ian was always very supportive. I have met some fabulous people and made some wonderful friends. Now, when I am asked, I say I am a quiltmaker. That's what I do.

TREE OF LIFE

187 cm x 193 cm, 1993

Picture perfect

ROBYN GINN

ANDREW PAYNE

The crowd of over two hundred and fifty women hushed as Robyn Ginn took the stage. Tucked under her arm were two of her picture quilts – what everyone had come to see. As Robyn began to share her thoughts and feelings about her quilts, a quiet pervaded the room as the women identified with her message and absorbed her explanation of her wondrous quilts:

In the Bible, Jeremiah reminds us that 'blessed is the man who trusts in the Lord and has made the Lord his hope and confidence. He is like a tree planted along a river bank with its roots reaching deep into the water – a tree not bothered by the heat nor worried by the long months of drought.' The tree reminds us that there are people like that who provide support for others, encouraging them to grow under their protection and allowing none of the trials of life to stop their own growing. Lots of different trees – all different types of people – surround the tree, and the dead-looking tree is dormant, waiting to begin to grow again. The hens are a reminder to me to 'give an egg a day' and always to be generous.

The richness of Robyn's words were echoed by her quilts which were designed to communicate, as well as to decorate, as were so many picture quilts of generations past.

Women have always used quilts to communicate their ideas, to celebrate an event, or simply to decorate the home. Appliqué, the process of cutting out shapes from one fabric and sewing it to another, has always been a very accessible medium for making pictures on quilts. Robyn Ginn celebrates this tradition, making appliqué quilts that tell stories:

I love needlework. For as long as I can remember, I have been making things with my hands. When I first started working, I bought a sewing machine (after I had bought a camera). I just loved to sew.

In 1979, Robyn was forced to return to hospital to undergo major surgery on her neck, an operation she had had three years previously and which required her to be a further six months in a full body plaster. The agony of this experience cannot be underestimated, particularly for such an active person who was always

89

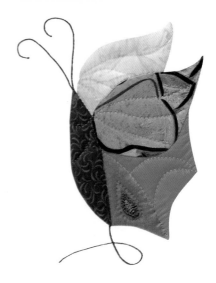

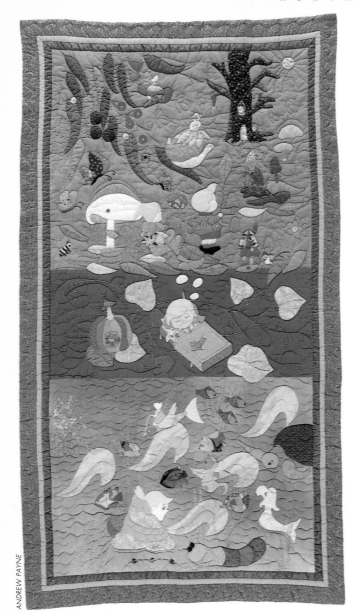

ANDREW PAYNE

FANTASY – A DREAMING (above), 121 cm x 206 cm, 1990
QUILTED BUTTERFLY (above right), 1987

busy with her hands. She realised her days of machine-work were over and she found the canvases for her tapestries too heavy to work on. When she was finally free from the cast and ready to return to normal living, Robyn found that all her friends were enjoying their freedom, playing tennis and doing aerobics:

> *Because I couldn't do any of these things, I went to the Embroiderers' Guild to perfect my embroidery stitches and there I was introduced to quilts. That first day, a lady came with a 'Trip Around the World' quilt. I thought it*

was the most beautiful thing I had ever seen. I had done patchwork before, just the squares, but I had never seen a quilt with wadding in it. Sadly, I thought I would never be able to make a full-size quilt because it would be too heavy. So I made pieces of quilts and blocks and gave them away. Then I read about quilt-as-you-go where each block is quilted before it is assembled into a full-size quilt. I thought I would give it a go.

At one of the meetings of the Embroiderer's Guild, Robyn met an American lady who said she was tired of seeing Australian quilts using American patterns and challenged Robyn to investigate original patchwork designs with an Australian theme:

> *Her challenge really got at me and it stuck. I went home and designed a series of blocks, based on Australian wildflowers, using folded paper.*

These designs were quite symmetrical and geometric, in keeping with the traditions of patchwork, but Robyn soon got bored with these and other traditional blocks using straight lines. Taking that step of saying 'I don't like this' allowed Robyn the freedom to move on to create her own designs. Using lots of curves in her drawings, she completed three quilts in quick succession, featuring hearts and pumpkins, butterflies and shells. Each quilt had a centre medallion, surrounded by blocks, each appliquéd with a different design, and was assembled using the quilt-as-you-go method. The appliqué was done in the old-fashioned way by marking the right side of the fabric with a pencil, then turning the seam allowance under and basting. Robyn does not mark the background fabric so that she can move or rearrange the elements in her design as she wishes.

The quilts Robyn makes today use these same techniques. When there is a shape with several pieces, such as the butterfly, she assembles them in her hand, before they are applied to the background. Many of the shapes are quite large, providing a foil for the smaller pieces. The Queensland blue pumpkin has become a recurring theme in Robyn's quilts. 'This is to remind me that we all need balance in our lives, with food for both the body and the soul,' explains Robyn. Each of these larger shapes is made of many pieces, all basted and assembled in her hand before placement. The large pumpkin in 'And Then There Was My Garden' provides a balance with the smaller elements in the quilt, its tendrils spreading out over the garden, connecting all the elements together. In this quilt Robyn breaks with her pattern for medallion quilts and creates an interesting block pattern which demands that larger pieces be worked together by the quilt-as-you-go method:

ANDREW PAYNE

A BUTTERFLY'S GARDEN, *130 cm x 184 cm, 1991*

I think I was able to achieve so much when I first started quilting because I used quilt-as-you-go. It was *portable and I could take it to my quilting groups. I could sit down at night and see my progress and not get discouraged. Then I would happily pick it up the next night and continue on.*

The designs for her quilts are not copied from other sources, but emerge from Robyn's own imagination:

Often I will be doodling while on the phone and come back later to see that I have the beginnings of a fantastic bird or some other fantasy creature. I try to

ANDREW PAYNE

WHAT IS FREEDOM?, *225 cm x 273 cm, 1991*

encourage my students to develop their own creativity. They often don't feel they have the ability but, when I encourage them to begin with my designs and then make some small changes, they begin to see the possibilities. I want them to be free to design and to enjoy it.

Freedom is a recurring theme in Robyn's quilts. She feels she has been given complete freedom to explore her own creativity by her very supportive husband, Alan, who she says pays all the bills. The butterfly has become Robyn's symbol, a sign of freedom since she emerged from her cocoon of plaster. 'What is Freedom' is a quilt featuring a carousel horse, escaped from the carousel with nowhere to go. 'This is just like the person who goes in search of freedom,' explains Robyn, 'but they don't realise that there will be no happiness without achievement and no achievement without other people.'

Robyn loves to teach. Part of the joy of quiltmaking for her is getting to know the many students who cross her path and sharing the stories of her quilts with them.

Wherever I go, I have started a quilting group, usually held in my home. I like to help women and often find that when we are all sitting quilting, all the barriers are down. No-one wants to know what you do for a living. A grandmother may be sitting next to a new mum and have instant rapport and someone who is a

AND THEN THERE WAS MY GARDEN, *240 cm x 287 cm, 1987*

ANDREW PAYNE

doctor may learn from an uneducated person. I guess my greatest pleasure would be having someone I have taught, tell me that my quilts and their stories have made a difference in their lives.

Robyn's new quilt, 'Call Me Australian' was the first quilt she has made with students in mind. Tired of the Australian quilts that reflected other people's environments, like the Baltimore quilts, Robyn set about making a quilt that showcased her own memories. Each block is small and reproducible, and Robyn is keen to encourage others to develop their own memory quilt. The house in the middle is reminiscent of her grandmother's house and she was delighted that her brother recognised it, without its front steps and with an area under the house for the drays. Robyn has used her unique embroidery to depict her grandmother's cottage garden in the front of the house: 'There aren't a lot of stitches to choose from, so my stitches evolve and move around. For example, feathered chain is very structured. If you straighten it up and bring the chain closer together you can get canna stalks.' In the corners of the quilt are four smaller squares, each one recalling a part of Robyn's life. On one, the chooks that gave her grandma an egg a day again remind Robyn to be generous. On the second is the outside 'dunny' which used to be part of everyday life with its resident spider and toad. On the third is the hat, a reminder of the many Sundays Robyn attended church. The camphor laurel tree is in the last corner, part of our British heritage. All around the border, Robyn has appliquéd lantana, which she feels is taking over Australia. Each flower is heavily embroidered. Robyn achieves that solid look by working her embroidery onto a piece of matching fabric placed over the quilt fabric. This method ensures that there are no visible gaps in the embroidery and the effect is very dense. Embroidery is a feature of all Robyn's quilts with more and more embroidery being used in her most recent work.

Robyn is a very popular tutor and is in constant demand. While it is important for her students to learn about appliqué techniques and innovative embroidery stitches, many of them attend her classes to listen to the stories

ANDREW PAYNE

94

of the quilts and to reflect on Robyn's philosophy of life. Many have enjoyed reading about the picture quilts in her book *that Quilt has a Story*, self-published by Robyn so that she could retain control of the content and design. In her book, Robyn has recorded her thoughts about each of her

quilts. Through them we catch glimpses of the personalities of the people in her family and the importance of her faith, providing the cornerstone for her life. In her book, Robyn says:

> *I find quilting a fulfilling and rewarding thing to be doing, gradually discovering the truth 'that in quietness and confidence, He will be your strength'. I have observed many women produce wonderful work and their achievements have transformed their lives. Their most important hurdle? They just had to begin.*

CALL ME AUSTRALIAN *(left)*, 240 cm x 260 cm, 1995
Detail from Call Me Australian (above)

ANDREW PAYNE